Family & Friends' Guide to Domestic Violence

How to Listen, Talk, and Take Action When Someone You Care About Is Being Abused

From the Publishers:

It is with pride that Volcano Press is publishing Elaine Weiss. Her books demonstrate the great advances in the struggle against family violence that have taken place since we first published BATTERED WIVES in the early 1970s.

In those early days, a handful of feminists, scattered across the United States, were creating shelters for battered women—without funding, without community understanding, against great odds. It was a historic movement.

Today, we have the Violence Against Women Act (VAWA), which established an agency of the U.S. Department of Justice. In addition, there are many state domestic violence coalitions and a myriad of local programs to support battered women.

Still, ending domestic violence is an ongoing movement that must involve the entire community. We believe that FAMILY AND FRIENDS' GUIDE TO DOMESTIC VIOLENCE will help you to "Listen, Talk and Take Action When Someone You Care About is Being Abused."

—*Ruth Gottstein*, Publisher
—*Adam Gottstein*, Associate Publisher

Also by Elaine Weiss

Surviving Domestic Violence:
Voices of Women Who Broke Free (2000)

Family & Friends' Guide to Domestic Violence

How to Listen, Talk, and Take Action
When Someone You Care About
Is Being Abused

Elaine Weiss, Ed.D.

VOLCANO
· PRESS ·

www.volcanopress.com

Library of Congress Cataloging-in-Publication Data

Weiss, Elaine.
   The family and friends guide to domestic violence : how to listen,
   talk, and take action when someone you care about is being abused /
   by Elaine Weiss.—1st America pbk ed.
      p.   cm.
   ISBN 1-884244-22-X (pbk.)
   1. Family violence—United States. I. Title.
   HV6626.2.W417 2003
   362.82'92—dc21   2003004642

Cover design by Diane McIntosh
Cover image: Photodisc (RF), Tim Teebin, illustrator
Interior page design by Jeff Brandenburg/image-comp.com

Volcano Press, Inc.
P.O. Box 270
Volcano, CA 95689

Telephone: 209 296 4991
Orders only: 800 879 9636
Fax: 209 296 4995

For online catalog and ordering: www.volcanopress.com
E-mail: sales@volcanopress.com

First printing, Volcano Press, Inc. 2003
Printed in the United States of America

For Neal Whitman...
my husband, my dearest friend, the love of my life...
with all my heart

For an abused woman, leaving the relationship is never a single act.
It is always a process.
The process of escaping from domestic abuse is one of quiet strengthening.
It can happen so silently, over such a long period of time,
that you will be unaware of it.
You may even feel frustrated, because your words and actions
seem to be having no impact.
It seems as though nothing is happening.
She looks as though she is a passive participant in her life,
willing to swallow whatever her abuser dishes out.
But don't be too sure of that.

There is a parallel in the insect world.
Substantial energy is required for a moth to lift itself in flight.
The wing muscles must reach a certain critical temperature
before they can move the wings fast enough to let the moth fly.
Until that temperature is reached, flight is impossible.

Acknowledgments

The Persian poet Hada Bejar wrote, "The fragrance always stays in the hand that gives the rose." I have spent the past decade learning and growing as an advocate for domestic tranquility; many dear people have handed me roses along the way.

The University of Utah School of Medicine, by making me their "point person" on domestic violence, has given me the opportunity to reach hundreds of physicians, medical students, and other health care professionals. I particularly want to thank Dr. Michael Magill, Chairman of the Department of Family and Preventive Medicine, for welcoming me into his department. Thanks as well to School of Medicine colleagues Marc Babitz, Jan DeWitt, Leonard Haas, Leigh Neumayer, Osman Sanyer, Don Pedersen, Kathy Pedersen, and Gordon Smith.

To teach is to learn twice. Thank you to the many medical schools, teaching hospitals, professional organizations, and community groups who have invited me to speak and, as a result, to learn.

Thanks also to those who have shaped my thinking about domestic abuse: Brandy Farmer, Jacci Graham, Jan Graham, Linda and Rick Grimes, Julie Jonassen, Judy Kasten-Bell, Andy Klein, Beverly Krensky, Kris Knowlton, Randee Lefkow, Jenny Mackenzie, Lou Mueller, Amy Rubin, Asha Parekh, Sonia Salari, Diane Stuart, Laura Taylor, Linda Taylor, Shelly White, Brett Wilcox, Karen Wilson, Robin Winner, Joan Zorza, and all the wonderful people at the YWCA of Salt Lake City.

Thank you to my friends for their energizing hugs: Karen Anastasopoulos, Annalee Clark, Cathy Crawford, Helene Cuomo,

Barbara Fontaine, Rita Fordham, Paula Green Johnson, Beth Guss, Louine Holt, Laurel Hughes, Jane Hunt, Phyllis and Wayne Kelley, Susan Makov, Mary McCarthy, Audrey and Jack Whipple. A special thanks to Phyllis for the poems and prayers and to Susan for the lingering lunches.

I see Volcano Press as far more than a publisher: they have become family. Over the past year, I have come to know Ruth Gottstein as a woman of enormous strength, compassion, and a firm sense of vision. She is an inspiration. And whenever my energy flagged, an encouraging e-mail from Adam Gottstein would magically pop up on my computer screen. "Onward," his letters always close. So I went.

Stories are like seeds. They need to be scattered so they can take root far from where they began. I thank the hundreds of woman who generously shared their stories in person and via e-mail. I thank all their friends and family members whose questions inspired this book.

Finally, many thanks are due to my mother, Celia Weiss, for her intellectual and moral support. And, as always, to my husband Neal Whitman, the finest man I know, for his love, enthusiasm, encouragement, applause, and belief in my vision.

—*Elaine Weiss, Ed.D.*
Salt Lake City, Utah

Foreword

Elaine Weiss offers practical answers to extraordinarily complex questions raised by abuse. All of us want a world that is safe for women and children, but it's hard to know what to do when we or some one we care about needs help. *The Family & Friends' Guide to Domestic Violence* helps connect the vision of a better world with the imperfect day-to-day reality that is abuse. Weiss' personal understanding of the impact violence can have on one's life, and her ability to speak to all of us—including men—in a language we can understand, makes her work vital.

—*Esta Soler, Founder and President*
Family Violence Prevention Fund

Table of Contents

Getting Involved

*In the middle of one night, Miss Clavel turned
on her light, and said, "Something is not right!"*

— LUDWIG BEMELMANS, *Madeline*

People have many feelings about domestic abuse, especially if it is
happening to someone they care about. They feel shock, anger, sadness, and frustration. I hope this book will help you transform those
feelings into a new one, *compassion*. When you feel compassion, you
experience the life of another person in a visceral way, not in your
mind but somewhere in your gut. As you experience the suffering of
another, you are moved by that suffering to listen, talk, or take action.

This may be the first time in your life you have thought about
domestic abuse. Until someone you care about became trapped in an
abusive relationship, you had no reason to consider this dark subject.
Now and then you would see a story on the evening news. Now and
then you would read a newspaper headline. But these stories had no
personal connection to your life because they didn't describe anyone
you knew . . . until now.

Now you know someone dealing with domestic abuse: a coworker,
a neighbor, a relative, or a dear friend. Now you are searching for
answers. You are not alone in this search; everyone knows someone

whose life has been touched by domestic abuse. I know this is true. Because of my work as an advocate for abused women and their children, I meet the victims of domestic violence and I meet the people who care about them.

I have been writing and teaching about domestic violence for nearly a decade. Early on, I discovered how to make conversation at a social event come to a screeching halt. When someone asks what you do, you answer that you write and teach about domestic violence. There will be an immediate black hole of silence, followed by a frantic babble of voices.

Some people, threatened by the very idea of such a subject, immediately change the subject or make a silly joke. Others want to know more. "What causes domestic violence?" they ask. "Is there more abuse now than there once was? Whose fault is it?" I enter willingly into the conversation, always happy for the chance to educate, while knowing full well that eventually I will hear, "Why don't these women just leave?" Isn't it interesting that no one ever asks the more pertinent question: "Why don't these abusers just *stop*?" But putting that to one side, the more important point is this: Abused women *do* leave. They leave all the time. Against all odds, often at enormous risk, they leave.

Hundreds of women have trusted me with their stories of how they broke free of an abusive relationship. I am honored that they have allowed me to become the keeper of their stories. My life is richer for having met them. As a writer and teacher, I often use the words of these survivors, because I believe that they can enlighten us about the complexities of living with, and escaping from, an abusive relationship. One important lesson I have learned from women who broke free is that a well-chosen word or action from a worried colleague, friend, or family member made an important difference.

You may know for certain that your family member or friend is a victim of domestic violence. She may have told you. You may have seen it happen. You may even have experienced the horror of seeing someone you care about in a hospital bed. Or you may be lying awake in the middle of the night, like Miss Clavel, concerned that "something is not right" in the life of someone you know. So how can you tell if she is being abused?

You can't tell for sure unless you ask her. But even before you ask (more about starting this conversation in Chapter 5), you can get a pretty good idea by reflecting on things you have seen or heard. Unexplainable injuries are an obvious sign, though she may put energy into convincing you that she simply tripped. Other signs are much more subtle. For example, you may have noticed that she is distancing herself from people she once spent time with. As you reflect on her situation, it may occur to you that she has very little say in her life. Competent in most social settings, she becomes timid when her husband or boyfriend is around. He sometimes makes jokes at her expense...and she tolerates it. Occasionally, you get the uneasy feeling that she is slightly fearful.

Checklist 1 summarizes five warning signs of domestic abuse. *If you have observed any of these, then this book is for you.* Your family member or friend may be a victim of domestic abuse. And you can help.

CHECKLIST 1: WARNING SIGNS OF DOMESTIC ABUSE

WARNING SIGN	EXAMPLES
Her social relationships have narrowed	She has pulled away from people she used to see frequently. She cancels social plans at the last minute. If she is on the phone when he arrives home, she ends the call quickly. At social gatherings, she is quieter than she used to be, sticking close to him or studying his facial expressions.
He makes all the rules	He has convinced her to drop out of college so that she can help him build a new business. He decides where they live, how their children are disciplined, and even what outfits she can wear.
He puts her down	He teases her, makes her the butt of jokes, or subjects her to outright ridicule. He calls her by a vaguely insulting nickname. He criticizes her appearance. He undermines her authority with her children. He makes fun of her opinions, her family, her religion, or her ethnicity.
She is afraid	She tells you that there are problems at home but that they are her fault. You have seen him glare at her...and seen her flinch. You have overheard vicious arguments. You know that there are weapons in the house.
She has been injured	Your normally graceful relative or friend has suddenly become "accident-prone." She has bruises or injuries that do not match her explanations. She has taken to wearing shirts with long sleeves and high collars.

There may be another reason for you to read this book. Your friend or relative may not currently be in an abusive relationship but was a victim of domestic abuse at some point in her past. You may have known her at that time; you may even have tried to help. Or it may have happened long before you met. She might be reluctant to share any more than the bare facts of her history, worried that if you knew the details, you would think less of her. You may have been reluctant to ask, worried that you would be unable to handle the truth and that your discomfort might make things worse. "Let sleeping dogs lie," you may have thought. "Why stir it all up again?" And so she didn't tell, and you didn't ask, the two of you in unspoken collusion to bury her past. Now, perhaps, you are ready to consider this difficult subject. Because you care about her, you want to understand what the experience was like for her then and how it may be affecting her now.

Considering Domestic Abuse

Say the words "domestic abuse" and an image springs instantly to mind. A weak little mouse of a victim cowers in a corner of a rundown apartment while her drunken brute of a husband kicks the dog, smacks the kids, and pounds the stuffing out of her. She takes it because she doesn't know any better, because she was raised in a home where her father beat her mother. She'll never leave because she'd rather have an abusive guy than no guy at all.

Stereotypes do not spring out of thin air; your relative or friend may look very much like this woman. Or she may look completely different. She may be a librarian with a daughter in college and a son who teaches high school physics. She may be your running partner or the woman next door. She may be your sorority sister. She may be your mother. Her husband may indeed drink like a fish, or he may imbibe nothing stronger than espresso. How is this possible? Is your family member or friend an exception to the rule: the only educated, middle-class woman with an abusive husband or boyfriend? The problem with stereotypes is that they present a flattened view of reality. A woman's financial status, ethnicity, educational level, and religion do not immunize her against the possibility of being abused.

Domestic abuse is extremely complicated. It's not a photograph that registers the minute you look at it. It's three-dimensional. It's a piece of sculpture. You have to take the time to walk around it, studying it from different angles, if you want to understand what it's really like for a woman who is living with an abuser.

As you have begun to wander through the murky landscape of domestic abuse, you have probably asked yourself how such a thing could happen between two people who love each other. You are not naïve; you know that even the best relationships have their muddles. They are punctuated with misunderstandings, arguments, or even periods of bitter anger. So, in trying to understand domestic abuse, you may have concluded that it happens like this. A man's wife or girl-friend does something he doesn't like. He gets angry with her. He is a man with hot temper, so instead of dealing with the situation in a reasonable way, he loses control and hits her.

Right?

Wrong.

Domestic abuse is not anger gone haywire. It is, in fact, rarely caused by anger at all. The people who inflict domestic abuse do not have an "anger management" problem. (Some abusers *are* violent everywhere and truly cannot control their tempers. More about this in Chapter 4.) *Most* abusers are only abusive in private and only target their intimate partners and children. Here is a case in point. A popular baseball player is arrested for beating up his girlfriend. His punishment? One hundred hours of community service (because he's such a great role model for school children) and six months of anger management classes. Yet how does this same man act when he's on the baseball field? He certainly doesn't beat up the umpire who calls him out on strikes. In fact, he knows that if he even *brushes* the ump on his way back to the dugout, he will be tossed out of the game. Does this guy have an anger management problem? I don't think so! So, what's going on here?

Clearly, it's something pretty complicated. If you know someone who is being abused and want to help her get a handle on what to do about it, you will need to understand these complexities. This book will help.

Not All Bad Stuff Is Abuse

Before examining what abuse *is*, it is important first to clarify what abuse *is not*. Domestic abuse is not simply this week's fancy name for what once was called a match made in hell. "We used to just call these guys S.O.B.s," a friend mused recently. "Now I guess we call them abusers." I hate to correct my friends when they are so obviously trying to understand what I do for a living. But this is not a useful way to frame the issue, because if we call everything abuse, then nothing is abuse.

Not every S.O.B. is an abuser; not every match made in hell is an abusive relationship. For example, arguments *are not* domestic abuse. There are couples who rarely argue; there are other couples who argue frequently. In some relationships, a healthy argument clears the air. In other relationships, arguments are destructive. But even destructive arguments, even constant bickering is not the same as domestic abuse.

There are certainly bad relationships out there, relationships that are lacking in trust, intimacy, or common goals. There are relationships where one of the partners is blatantly unfaithful. There are marriages where husband and wife have not spoken a civil word to each other in years. But these marriages are not necessarily abusive. There are many other reasons, aside from domestic abuse, for a marriage to fall apart.

Then there are relationships where one partner uses a combination of physical, sexual, and psychological tactics to gain complete control over the other. The victims in these relationships live in constant fear of saying or doing the wrong thing. These are the true abusive relationships.

What About Gender?

As you read this book, you will see that I refer to perpetrators of domestic abuse as "he" and victims as "she." For most of you, this will accurately describe your friend or relative's situation. For a few of you, it will not. For example, your sister might have a female partner who flies into jealous rages. Your nephew might have a male lover who routinely beats him. Your son might be afraid of his wife. But it is important to recognize that these cases are the exception. Most of the time, men abuse women.

Do women hit, kick, bite, push, and even kill their intimate partners? Yes, they do. But, to quote domestic violence expert Andy Klein, a columnist for *Domestic Violence Prevention*, "...it isn't the same domestic violence that the overwhelming majority of men get arrested for." In most cases, a woman cannot injure a man as seriously as he can injure her. In addition, the motivation for a woman to hurt a man is often self-defense, retaliation, protection of her children, or a desire to escape. It is not usually part of a deliberate campaign to control, isolate, intimidate, and humiliate her partner. A single act of physical violence is rarely accompanied by an ongoing pattern of psychological abuse. Finally, a woman's violence toward her male partner is not generally out of proportion to his actions. If he slaps her, she may slap him back, but she is unlikely to up the ante much beyond that. Men are far more likely to do this than women. As one woman told me, "I would get so fed up that I'd punch him in the arm, and then he'd spend the next hour beating the crap out of me."

Even though men abuse women far more than women abuse men, this does not mean that the problem here is men! I emphasize this because it is important to distinguish the minority of abusive men from the majority of men in general. I learned this lesson the hard way. When I first began teaching medical students about domestic violence, I noticed that the women in the audience followed my words eagerly and peppered me with questions. Meanwhile, the men sat strangely silent, their hands clasped tightly over their private parts. Medical students are generally a noisy, challenging bunch, so it was pretty hard to miss that half the class was not with me. Half the class felt attacked.

My goal is not to attack an entire gender. I firmly believe that the difficulty lies not with men but with abusers. Although it is true that most abusers are men, it is also true that most bank robbers are men. Just as most men don't rob banks, most men do not beat up their wives or girlfriends. Most men do not endanger their children. In their view of human relations, violence toward family members is simply not an option.

If your family member or friend is a man or woman in a same-sex relationship, or if he is a man who is being abused by a woman, you will still find the information in this book helpful. Whether a victim is male or female, the fact remains that domestic abuse is a dreadful betrayal of trust. Its victims suffer devastating emotional pain. They feel ashamed, heartbroken, and filled with self-doubt. Ultimately, domestic abuse is not a gender issue. It is a human rights issue.

Making a Difference

It's hard to know what to do when someone you care about is in an abusive relationship. Do you ask about it? What if you're wrong? Do you offer to help? What if you're accused of interfering? Do you take action? What if you put yourself or your family at risk? As one woman wrote to me, "My daughter's fiancé has already convinced her that she has no friends and that it is her family who is making her unhappy. I find it difficult to understand what kind of hold he has on her, but I do see her becoming more and more alienated from people she has always loved and trusted, while at the same time becoming dependent on him for even simple things such as what foods she can eat or what kinds of clothes she can wear. I have tried to let her know that it is hard for me to understand—she knows how we feel, but I haven't wanted to further alienate her by being demanding myself. I want her to know that she can always come home if she needs to, but is there anything else I can do that will make a difference?"

Family and friends can make an enormous difference to someone who is trapped in the web of domestic abuse. Your involvement may be as simple—and powerful—as a well-thought-out sentence spoken at just the right time. It may be a longer-term commitment. This book explains the many ways you can help someone you care about.

There are other people who can help, too. You are not alone in this effort. There are domestic violence advocates and counselors. There are police, lawyers, doctors, religious leaders, and social service employees. The support they can offer is important. The support you can offer is different—but no less important. Because of your special relationship with the victim, you can help in ways no one else can. You also have to walk a much finer line. Your sister's doctor can ask her if she feels safe at home. She may open up to him, or she may become offended and never return to his office. But if you ask your sister the identical question, you risk the entire relationship. No wonder you feel torn!

I truly believe that people want to do the right thing. They just don't always know what the right thing is. A very nice elderly lady once approached me in tears after I made a presentation in her city. "My daughter and her husband had five little children when she came to me for help," she whispered. "I told her she had to figure out a way to make her marriage work. I thought that because he wasn't hitting her, she wasn't being abused. How could I have done that to her?" When a mother tells her daughter to stay in an abusive marriage "for the sake of the children," when a sister tells her brother that "a real man wouldn't let his wife be such a bitch," when a college student tells her roommate, "If you don't break up with that turkey, I've had it with you," they are not being malicious. They are trying to do something—anything—to make a bad situation better.

Other people take the opposite approach. They say nothing at all. Some are afraid of saying the wrong thing. What, after all, *do* you say when you catch an embarrassing glimpse of your niece's husband shaking a fist at her in the back seat of your car? Others are reluctant to intrude on a private matter. My friend Gloria has two sons whose wives have never seen eye-to-eye. Gloria has wisely decided that her best course of action is to stay out of it. "I wear beige and keep my mouth shut," she quips. Gloria's philosophy works well to smooth over most family wrinkles. But a victim of domestic abuse does not see your silence as an attempt to give her privacy. She sees it as disapproval, acceptance, or lack of interest. It makes her feel that she is imagining things. It makes her feel invisible.

If you have a family member, friend, client, coworker, or neighbor who you suspect is in an abusive relationship, you may have already tried to help, or you may have kept silent for fear of making things worse. Chapters 2, 3, and 4 will teach you about domestic abuse, so that you can understand the complexities of her life. If she was in an abusive relationship earlier in her life, these chapters will help you understand that part of her history. In Chapters 5 through 7, you will learn the words and actions that can make a difference as she works to break free. Chapter 8 will show how you can remain involved by providing ongoing support to a family member or friend who has escaped from an abuser, either recently or long ago.

For an abused woman, leaving the relationship is never a single act. It is always a process. The process of escaping from domestic abuse is one of quiet strengthening. It can happen so silently, over such a long period of time, that you will be unaware of it. You may even feel frustrated, because your words and actions seem to be having no impact. It seems as though nothing is happening. She looks as though she is a passive participant in her life, willing to swallow whatever her abuser dishes out. But don't be too sure of that.

There is a parallel in the insect world. Substantial energy is required for a moth to lift itself in flight. The wing muscles must reach a certain critical temperature before they can move the wings fast enough to let the moth fly. Until that temperature is reached, flight is impossible. So here is what you can see on a cool autumn evening in your backyard. There are the moths, sitting quietly, all over your lawn furniture. Since they are not moving, you imagine they are passive. But they are not. They are flexing their flight muscles without actually moving their wings, until they have worked up enough heat to take off. Then suddenly, with seemingly no effort or warning, their wings flutter and they are gone.

The support you offer, the time you spend listening and reflecting on what you hear, the actions you take, all propel your friend or family member further along in the process of breaking free of domestic abuse and going on with her life.

Understanding Domestic Abuse

What's Love Got to Do With It?

A lawyer who attended one of my presentations described a client who, he said, "made a decision to enter into an abusive marriage." In my opinion, this woman should get herself a new lawyer. As long as her attorney views her current situation as the result of a decision she made, he will be unable to help her. Everything he says will be colored by his conviction that domestic abuse is a choice. This is the attitude of all complacent critics who blame the victims of rape, abuse, robbery, and any other unwelcome and unwished-for assaults.

"What's love got to do with it?" Tina Turner belted out in 1984, nearly a decade after she ended her marriage to Ike Turner, her singing partner and abusive husband. Her story, brilliantly portrayed by Angela Basset in the 1993 movie of the same name, painted a devastating picture of physical, sexual, and psychological violence.

So what's love got to do with domestic abuse? Nothing! When I teach, I wear a heart-shaped pendant, part of an awareness campaign funded by the Liz Claiborne Company several years ago. The words "LOVE IS NOT ABUSE" are etched on one side of the heart. A flip of the chain reveals the back of the heart and the remainder of the message: "ABUSE IS NOT LOVE."

Occasionally in life, we knowingly put ourselves at risk. We do so out of a feeling of love, love for an individual, a country, or an ideal. A mother runs in front of a speeding car, braving the onrush of metal to pull her toddler to safety. A couple adopts a child with a serious medical condition. A high school graduate chooses a career in fire fighting. A social worker counsels gang members in an inner-city housing project. A medical team sets up tents in a country diminished by fighting and famine.

The victim of domestic abuse generally *does not* deliberately put herself at risk. She does not choose dangerous love…she chooses love. It is true that some women knowingly enter into a relationship with a man who has been abusive, hoping perhaps that he will change over time. Some women marry, not for love but for expediency. Some are forced into marriage. For most women, though, the danger comes as a shock, out of nowhere. One woman described it to me like this: "I had known this man for 10 years. He was my absolute best friend for 10 years before we got married. I had never seen him angry. It was a very close relationship and I could talk to him about anything. But the minute I married him, I no longer had a best friend…I had a controller."

Comprehending the Incomprehensible

I am asking you to do something hard. I am asking you to share someone else's nightmare. If you want to support a victim of domestic abuse, you have to understand what the experience is like for her. You may have been a victim of domestic abuse yourself; if so, her experience will be all too familiar. If not, it will be difficult to put yourself in her place.

Many people try to understand an abusive relationship by comparing it to their own relationships. After all, every couple argues. Consider for a moment your most poisonous argument with a person you love. Relive your actions as the situation escalated. Perhaps you yelled or slammed a door. Perhaps you stormed out of the house, got into your car, and drove away in a righteous huff. It would be tempting to believe that when a relationship is abusive, instead of doing one of those things, someone throws a punch or a chair, or fires a gun. You might think that an abusive relationship is just like your relationship…except that *you* can control yourself and an abuser cannot.

But, while a punch, a flung chair, and a gunshot are certainly examples of domestic abuse, they do not tell the complete story of an abused woman's experience. *Domestic abuse is a constant state of affairs.*

A victim of domestic violence is always on her toes. What was right yesterday may be wrong today. "Is today the day he loves meatloaf," she agonizes, "and I'd better make it for dinner; or is today the day he hates meatloaf, and I'm a bitch for cooking it?" Meatloaf may not seem like a big deal. If he wants it, he'll ask for it. If he doesn't, he'll go out for pizza. In your house, sure. In her house, probably not.

If you want to comprehend the incomprehensible, you must conceive of a home where there is a rule about everything…and the rules keep changing. You must imagine a relationship where differences of opinion are never tolerated and compromises are never negotiated. You must picture a man who insists that he be obeyed at all times, immediately and without question. You must visualize a woman who puts all her energy into "getting it right." Only there is no way she can ever get it right. Because he needs her to get it wrong.

A student at my medical school, clearly troubled, raises her hand during my presentation on domestic violence intervention with patients. "Surely you aren't saying that abusers do this *on purpose?*" she says. This is difficult to fathom, I know. Bad enough to know that people treat other people this way, nearly impossible to believe that such treatment is intentional. How else, though, to explain abuser actions?

Lawyer and domestic violence expert Joan Zorza has many personal examples of the premeditated nature of violence against women. "Being a legal services lawyer," she wrote to me recently, "my clients were all poor. When I started doing this work, men frequently cut the phone lines or smashed the phone during a fight so the woman couldn't call the police or anyone else for help. But once the phone company divested and he knew he would get stuck paying to have the lines rewired or get a new phone, *not one man cut his own phone line or smashed his own phone.* Instead they locked the phone in the trunks of their cars when they went to work in the mornings, or carefully unscrewed the phones from the wall before beginning a beating. Before this, I, too hadn't believed that the abuse was premeditated, but this made clear to me that the men were choosing excuses to go after their victims, not getting angry and out of control."

Domestic Abuse Is a Campaign

Domestic abuse is not just a curse, a slap, or even a severe beating. It is an intentional, ongoing, purposeful effort. In other words, it is a campaign. Every four years in this country, we witness presidential campaigns. Our nation is treated to advertisements, billboards, stump speeches, and televised debates, all aimed at a single purpose: to convince us to cast our vote for Politician A instead of Politician B.

Campaigns are intentional. No one undertakes a political campaign by accident. In a relationship, accidents can and do happen; we must not rush to judgment, calling all hurtful actions abuse. The key word is "intentional"; we are not talking about unthinking rudeness. I've done plenty of that in my life. So have you. We're talking about behavior that is *calculated* to do damage. A hurtful remark or a shouted insult might be accidental. Even a single push or a single slap in the heat of an argument might be accidental...though it is certainly inappropriate. However, when pushes, slaps, shouts, threats, insults, jeers, accusations, punches, jealous rages, bites, pinches, unreasonable demands, curses, and rapes are a constant presence in the relationship, then this is no accident. The abuser has mounted a campaign.

Campaigns are ongoing. If you want to be president, you cannot run a single television ad in January and anticipate that you will receive a vote from anyone except your mother. An abuser's campaign is ongoing as well. A better term might be relentless. Not that the victim is being punched in the nose every day. In fact, the abuser may never punch her in the nose. Or he might punch her in the nose one time early in the relationship and never need to do so again, because he has proven that he is capable of assaulting her. Even with no physical violence whatsoever, victims feel they are trapped in the center of a minefield. They do not know where the land mines are buried, so they tiptoe gingerly, one careful step at a time, trying to shift as little weight as possible, always alert to the possibility that a careless move might trigger an explosion.

Campaigns are purposeful. The purpose of a presidential campaign is to win the election. The purpose of the abuser's campaign is to win the right to control the relationship. This notion of control gets a bit tricky, though, because all of us like a certain amount of control.

For example, in my house, I have strong opinions about where the dishes are placed in the dishwasher. My husband Neal has learned that when he loads the dishwasher (which he does, bless him, after every meal), I am likely to stroll past the open door and tweak a few plates and mugs. It's silly. But it's a harmless quirk, so he tolerates it. For his part, Neal has strong opinions about what time we should leave the house to arrive on time at the theater. By the time he accounts for every eventuality, including avalanches and monsoons, we are at least 30 minutes early. It's silly. But it's a harmless quirk, so I tolerate it.

In a healthy relationship, control is negotiated. In an abusive relationship, the abuser needs to have it all.

Abuser Tactics

A presidential campaign has an overall purpose: win the election. It also has *tactics*, specific actions that will put the candidate in the oval office. Since the abuser's purpose is to achieve control over the relationship, it makes sense that he will enlist a variety of tactics to achieve that purpose. Some of these tactics are physical. Many are not. That is why you may never see your family member or friend with a black eye, a broken arm, or a knife wound.

What kinds of tactics do abusers use? Everyone is familiar with the noisiest tactics; these are the ones that make the evening news—a child's kidnapping, a high-speed chase, a tragic hostage situation, a multiple murder/suicide. Many tactics, though, are so quiet as to seem negligible. And they are negligible unless viewed against the backdrop of the entire relationship, each abusive act magnified by the rest, until the collective group becomes, over time, too much to bear.

An abuser tends to use the tactics that work, taking into account his victim's specific vulnerabilities. We are *all* vulnerable to some extent. We all have things we don't like about ourselves. For me, it's the size of my hips and my lack of athletic ability. Don't ever invite me to join your game of beach volleyball. My serves are feeble, pathetic little chops, and I have an unfortunate tendency to duck when the ball comes my way. For other people, areas of vulnerability might be lack of a college degree, or crooked teeth, or shyness, or fear of heights. In most relationships, the person we love is sensitive to our vulnerabilities. The husband or boyfriend of a shy woman will stick by her side at parties until he is sure she has met a few people. The partner of someone who is afraid of heights would never make a reservation at the restaurant that revolves atop the Seattle Space Needle.

But abusers *use* these vulnerabilities. Think of it as "bad empathy."

One woman told me, "My husband kept all our bank accounts in his name. Whenever I needed money to pay bills, I had to ask him. It was really demeaning, so I told him I wanted a joint account. He told me I was too stupid to balance a checkbook and he bought me everything I wanted, so what was I complaining about?" This may not seem like such a big deal to you. Why didn't she tell him that that she was perfectly capable of balancing a checkbook, thank you very much, and that he was being an annoying jerk? She didn't do any of that because she had never done particularly well academically, had dropped out of high school during her senior year, and always worried that she did not measure up intellectually. Her husband used that vulnerability to grab control of the money and make her feel incompetent. Notice that he didn't hit her. But he managed to acquire complete control of their finances, one of many tactics that abusers use to achieve control in a relationship.

Another woman put it like this: "Whenever we were out with other people, I was on pins and needles because I expected to be humiliated about something I had done." This woman was fairly quiet. She had never been able to make friends easily. Like a heat-seeking missile, her boyfriend targeted this vulnerability, using her shyness to embarrass her in front of other people. As she retreated into herself, he was able to keep her isolated from other people. He never resorted to so obvious a tactic as forbidding her to go out without him. He simply arranged it so she had no friends to go with.

A third woman shared a particularly grim tactic. "My husband," she reported, "used to say that if I didn't shape up, he would have me committed to a mental institution. He said nobody would believe me because he was a prominent businessman and I was just a kindergarten teacher." This woman's father had a schizophrenic cousin who had been institutionalized from his mid-thirties until his death. For her, mental illness was a fear both tangible and fully possible. It was no coincidence that her husband chose this particular threat to keep her in line. He knew it would scare her. That's why he did it.

CHECKLIST 2:
ABUSERS USE A WIDE RANGE OF TACTICS TO ACHIEVE CONTROL

CONTROL THROUGH CRITICISM

• My partner never gives me positive support. Even his compliments are back-handed: "This is the first decent meal you've cooked in months."

• When we're out with family and friends, I'm always nervous because I never know when he'll pick on me about something I've done.

• My partner says he can help me fix my character defects. Then he makes lists of what's wrong with me and tells me I need to see a psychiatrist.

CONTROL THROUGH ISOLATION

• Whenever I want to go out, my partner always picks that time to start a fight.

• If I make a new friend at work or in the neighborhood, my partner always finds something wrong with her.

• My partner told everyone in the neighborhood that I'm hooked on pain pills. Now nobody believes me when I try to tell them that I'm afraid of him.

CONTROL THROUGH MONEY

• My partner won't give me a household allowance, so whenever I need money I have to ask him for it.

• My partner always reminds me that I could never live so well without him.

• My partner makes me cash my paycheck and turn it over to him. If I refuse to do it, he gets scary.

CONTROL THROUGH MIND GAMES

• My partner says cruel things and then says I'm too sensitive and can't take a joke.

• My partner tells my family that he is the victim and that I am the abuser. He's always so sweet to them, I'm afraid they will start to believe it.

• When I try to have a serious talk, my partner says, "You're hysterical. Calm down." He treats me like I'm upset when I'm not.

CONTROL THROUGH DECISION MAKING

• My partner does the grocery shopping because he says I'm too stupid to pick the right food.

• My partner picks out all my clothes, he says, because I have lousy taste and he knows what outfits suit me.

• My partner says all my relatives are a bad influence on me. He only lets me spend holidays with his family.

CONTROL THROUGH JEALOUSY

- When we are at a party and I talk to a man, I always have to keep an eye out for the expression on my partner's face.
- When I put on an outfit that looks good on me, my partner says I look like a tramp and makes me change clothes.
- If I come home late, my partner accuses me of having an affair.

CONTROL THROUGH CHILDREN

- My partner tells the children that I'm a bad mother, so that they'll be on his side.
- My partner threatens to tell Social Services that I'm an unfit mother if I don't do what he wants.
- My partner says that if I ever leave him, he will fight for full custody of our kids. Since he has a better job than I do, I'm afraid he'll succeed.

CONTROL THROUGH BLAME

- My partner says that he can't stay sober because I don't keep the house clean and the kids quiet.
- My partner says he wouldn't go after other women if I were thinner, prettier, smarter, and sexier.
- My partner tells me that if I worked outside the home, he'd have more respect for me.
- My partner tells me that he'd treat me better if I would stay at home with our children.

CONTROL THROUGH VERBAL THREATS

- When we have a fight, my partner tells me that I'm "acting like a nutcase." He says if I don't shape up, he'll have me committed to a mental institution.
- My partner says that if I ever leave him, he'll kill himself and I'll be responsible.
- My partner says he'll tell INS that I use cocaine. I'm afraid of being deported.

CONTROL THROUGH SEX

- My partner forces me to wear clothes that he thinks are sexy. I don't like being out in public dressed that way.
- My partner wants me to have sex the way they do it in porn movies. When I object, he says I'm frigid.
- My partner forces me to have sex against my will. He says it isn't rape because we are a couple.
- My partner refuses to use a condom during sex. I know he goes with other women, and I'm afraid of getting sick.

CONTROL THROUGH PHYSICAL THREATS

• My partner blocks the door so I can't leave during a fight.

• Once when I had an operation, he refused to bring me any food or get my prescriptions filled for three days. I was afraid I'd die, and nobody would know that he had done it.

• The last time I tried to get away from my partner, he stalked me for weeks. Eventually I got so afraid, I came home again.

• My partner likes to hold me against the wall with one hand and punch his other fist against the wall close to my head.

• My partner drives recklessly whenever he is angry with me. I'm afraid to get in the car with him, but he says I'm making a big deal over nothing.

CONTROL THROUGH PHYSICAL ASSAULT

• My partner throws things at me. He says if I call the police they'd just laugh at me, because I always duck in time so I don't have any bruises.

• My partner beats my head against the floor. He doesn't stop until I pretend to pass out.

• My partner kicks me, shoves me, bites me, pushes me, and punches me.

• My partner once strangled me. I passed out, but since I didn't have a bruise, he denied doing it.

• My partner once attacked me with a butcher knife. Another time he pushed me out of a moving car.

Checklist 2 shows some common abuser control tactics. (It is by no means all encompassing; throughout this book, you will find other examples of how abusers manipulate, frighten, and damage their victims.) I would hesitate to call any *single* instance of these domestic abuse except, of course, for coerced sex, physical threats, or physical force. However, in an abusive relationship, the tactics shape themselves into a *pattern*. For example, one abuser may use a combination of verbal threats (announcing his intention to kill himself if his partner leaves), jealousy (accusing his partner of having an affair with her boss), and physical threats (driving recklessly). Another abuser may use a combination of money (pocketing her welfare check), criticism (public ridicule), mind games (shaking his head in innocent wonder when she complains about his public ridicule), and physical violence (pushing her down the basement stairs). Also notice that some tactics cross over. For example, although regulating how frequently she can

see her parents is a form of decision making, it is also an isolation tactic. If he can isolate her from her friends and relatives (including you),
then he gets to make the rules.

Physical attacks are the most obvious control tactic. Your family
member or friend may have suffered dreadful beatings at the hands of
her husband or boyfriend. You may know all about these attacks,
because their physical manifestations—bruises, broken bones, or knife
wounds—were impossible to ignore. You may even have been the one
to drive her to the emergency room. Or you may know nothing about
it. Many abusers assault strategically, hurting their victims in ways
that look accidental or leaving bruises that can be hidden by clothing.
For example, victims report being burned with hot water, deliberate
attacks that can easily be dismissed as clumsy kitchen accidents. They
report being punched viciously and repeatedly in the abdomen, leaving huge bruises that vanish every morning when they dress for work.
They report being strangled, which often leaves no bruises at all. "I
could kill you if I wanted to," their abusers seem to be saying. "Next
time, I might just do it."

Physical threats can be as powerful a control tactic as physical violence...and threats leave no scars, no purple bruises, no evidence for
police or lawyers. Physical intimidation goes far beyond the threat of
a future physical assault. A man traps his wife in their tiny bathroom,
puts one hand on her chest to press her against the wall, and then
punches holes in the wall beside her head with his free fist. The message is clear: Look how easy it is for me to do this to the wall; if I
wanted to, I could do it to you.

I consider a threat of suicide to be a physical threat, and it is not a
threat I take lightly. I heard the following story from a man who works
the hotline at his city's shelter for battered women. The caller's voice
was hesitant. "I'm sorry to bother you," she whispered. "I probably
shouldn't even be calling the shelter. It's not like my husband beats me
up. He's never laid a hand on me. But whenever I do something that
makes him mad, he loads his pistol, puts it to his head, and says he'll
blow his brains out unless I apologize. So, of course, I do." You may
be thinking that this woman would be a lot better off if her husband
made good on his threat. True, a family member's suicide leaves the
survivors deeply scarred, but at least his wife would be free...and safe.
The unfortunate truth is that when an abuser takes his own life, he

often murders his victim first. When considering the victim's safety, a subject that will be addressed later in this chapter, *the abuser's threat of suicide must be taken as seriously as a threat of homicide.*

Seeing the Pattern

It is important to recognize that the complete pattern of abuser tactics only becomes clear over time. As you think back to early conversations you may have had with your friend or relative, you may recall a time when she said something like "He's awfully critical." Was this a clue that you missed? No. All of us have been critical at one time or another. There is a huge difference, though, between an occasional critical remark and a wearying onslaught of relentless criticism coupled with jealousy, physical threats, isolation, and so on.

How does an abused woman see the pattern of control tactics within her relationship? The answer is that she generally does not. You may decipher the pattern long before she does. It is difficult to see the picture when you are in the frame. There is an artist whose canvas is the tilled soil; living plants comprise the colors in his palette. In several acres of Iowa farmland he once planted the Mona Lisa. Visitors who wandered through the tended beds saw nothing but flowers, leaves, stems, and bark; the famous woman with the elusive smile could only be seen from an airplane.

It takes an abused woman time to recognize that her partner's insults, threats, manipulation, mind games, blame, and occasional physical attacks are not random acts but tactics in a campaign to gain control of the relationship. One woman compared the process to assembling a jigsaw puzzle. She told me, "You know one puzzle piece doesn't make a whole lot of sense. In fact, maybe it says nothing. So although his abuse was progressive, what also was progressive inside of me was those puzzle pieces. Once I got enough of them to see his face for what it really was, I think maybe that's when I could leave."

I believe the process of assembling the jigsaw puzzle pieces slowly and carefully, one piece at a time, gave this woman the strength she needed to leave her abusive husband. There are many reasons why abused women leave. Seeing the pattern is one. Right now, though, you are probably *not* wondering why women leave—you are wondering why they stay!

Why Does She Stay?

What would make a victim of abuse stay beyond the first insult, the first jealous rage, the first raised fist? This is a sensible question. I'm sure you've asked yourself this question many times. Were you in her shoes, you think to yourself, you would walk out at the first sign of trouble. Since *you* would and *she* hasn't, it's mighty tempting to wonder what's wrong with *her*.

There are many reasons why an abused woman remains with an abuser. If you want to support a victim of domestic abuse, you must understand the barriers standing in her way. You must also recognize the barriers standing in *your* way, the myths about domestic abuse that may keep you from fully understanding her situation.

The Self-Esteem Myth

You may perhaps have theorized that your friend or relative suffers from low self-esteem. Low self-esteem got her *into* the relationship, so this theory goes; therefore, the way to get her *out* of it is to raise her self-esteem. The problem with this theory is that it confuses cause and effect. Yes, many abused women suffer from low self-esteem while they are trapped within the confines of an abusive relationship. But there is no evidence that the majority of domestic abuse victims had low self-esteem *before* they were in an abusive relationship, or that they will continue to have low self-esteem *after* they get out of the relationship.

Our self-esteem is based on how well we can assess ourselves. Someone with high self-esteem will achieve clear successes, receive positive messages, and therefore believe that he or she is loved, competent, and successful. The success and positive message might be a red star on a spelling test, a job promotion, or the Nobel Peace Prize; a person with high self-esteem will absorb the message and feel just dandy. Someone with low self-esteem will feel anything but dandy. This person may achieve the same successes, may get the same positive messages, but in spite of this, believes that he or she is unloved, incompetent, and a failure.

This is how self-esteem works, assuming that the messages we receive from the people around us are honest. Most of us, thankfully, *do* receive honest messages. But for an abused woman, the messages she receives *are not* honest, so her sense of herself becomes distorted.

Her abuser devalues and shames her. No matter what she accomplishes in life, it is never good enough. Why would he say such things, she thinks, if they weren't true? She must be missing something. She must not be as competent as she thought. No matter how strong her sense of self when she entered the relationship, life with an abuser will take its toll. Eventually, she may lose her ability to judge who she really is.

Do abused women suffer from low self-esteem? Many do. After years of abuse, so would you! But this does not mean she had low self-esteem before she met him. Her problem is not that her self-esteem is low; the solution is not that her self-esteem must be raised. Her problem is that she is living with a person whose goal is to whittle away at her sense of herself, so that she eventually believes she cannot function without him.

The Violent Childhood Myth

Another misunderstanding many people have about domestic abuse is that all victims were raised in violent homes. The fact is, although some abused women saw domestic abuse at home, others barely heard an angry word. Also, although some women who witnessed domestic abuse as children repeat the pattern in their adult life, others do not. Daughters growing up in abusive families split into two roughly equal groups: those who recognize abuse, know they want nothing to do with it, and get out fast if they see it; and those who feel that abuse is a woman's lot in life.

A friend describes a conversation with a 17-year-old whose boyfriend beat and raped her, then threatened to kill her if she testified against him. The teenager told my friend that her father abused her mother, her grandfather had abused her grandmother. My friend ponders the sadness that violence is a learned behavior. This poor girl, seeing the women in her family being beaten, thinks this is the way life works. "That's why women choose violent men," my friend proclaims. "They've been programmed by their experiences as children." I try not to jump down her throat, but I do tell her about the women I've interviewed who never witnessed violence until they witnessed their own. I tell her about Lucy, who was so unprepared for her husband's punch that she didn't know to duck.

So where does this leave us? Women are abused because they grew up with abuse, because they believe that "that's just the way men act." And women are abused because they *didn't* grow up with abuse, because they *don't* know enough to protect themselves from an approaching fist. If my math is correct, that's 100 percent of all abused women!

The Psychological Defect Myth

In the past, when you heard about a woman in an abusive relationship, you may have assumed immediately that this was a woman with psychological problems, who has gone from one bad relationship to another—that, for some deep-seated, unfathomable reason, this woman *wants* to pick the wrong kind of guy.

This kind of woman is certainly out there. But they represent a tiny percentage of abused women. We remember these unrepresentative women precisely *because* they are so memorable. Experts in the field of medical decision making call this the "availability heuristic." That is, we remember only the dramatic, memorable cases: drugs, knives, bad guy after bad guy after bad guy. In the case of women who repeat abusive relationships, these same women typically repeat other bad decisions in their lives: drug use, risky sexual behavior, criminal activity, and other bad choices. Partnering with violent men may be only one of many bad paths they tread.

It is frustrating to be the friend, relative, neighbor, or coworker of a woman who repeatedly makes poor choices. And her situation certainly will be memorable, precisely because of your level of frustration. But chances are, the person you care about *does not* fit into this category. The overwhelming majority of women who have escaped from an abusive relationship are actually *hypervigilant*, determined to avoid another one. The explanation that abused women want to be abused simply does not hold water. But the few who appear that way are memorable.

There may be many reasons why your friend or family member stays. But you can safely assume that her reason *is not* due to a psychological defect that leaves her wanting to be abused by the man she loves. In fact, if you take the time to listen, you will find that her reasons are eminently sensible.

Reason #1: Fear

I have a colleague who runs court-ordered batterer treatment groups. These are weekly sessions for convicted wife-beaters, men who have been arrested, brought to trial, and given the option of six months in jail or 12 months of weekly sessions with two facilitators and 10 to 20 other batterers. Most, for obvious reasons, choose batterer treatment over jail. My colleague once asked a group participant, "What would happen if your wife hit you as hard as she possibly could?" The man replied, "I'd laugh." Then my colleague asked, "What would happen if *you* hit *her* as hard as *you* possibly could?" And the man answered, "She'd die."

We would all prefer not to be reminded that domestic abuse sometimes ends in death. It's a frightening thought. But even though many women do get away safely, the fact is that breaking free of domestic abuse is dangerous. A woman is at most risk of being seriously injured or killed in the six months after she leaves than at any other time in the relationship. This is true even if she has already been badly hurt during the relationship. Chances are good that she will be hurt worse if she leaves. It is also true even if there has been very little physical violence in the relationship. This makes sense when you consider that most abuse is all about control. As long as an abuser maintains control over the victim, the victim may actually be pretty safe. But once she leaves, the abuser loses control. Some abusers, faced with this possibility, try to destroy their victims. Some, sadly, succeed.

Many women in abusive relationships have heard threats from their abusers for years. "If I can't have you, life won't be worth living," an abuser may have said. "I'll put a gun to my head and it will be your fault." Or, more chilling for its singsong delivery, is the statement, "Go ahead—move out. Bye-bye. I hope you'll enjoy taking your meals through a feeding tube." Between the threats themselves and the news stories proving that these threats are not idle, it is no wonder that an abused woman is afraid. She may decide that she is safer staying put than attempting to escape. And she may be right.

If a woman feels that she has a safe place to go, where her abuser will be unable to reach her, she is more likely to leave him. Unfortunately, no abused woman's safety can be guaranteed. But there have been vast improvements over the past years. Many community resources exist that can help an abused woman implement a plan for her children's safety and her own. Chapter 6 describes these resources in detail.

Reason #2: Children

Many abused women have children with their abusers. In some cases, these children are at physical risk. They are always at emotional risk. Abused women with children are particularly vulnerable as they struggle to achieve the impossible, to reconcile two mutually exclusive needs. Should she leave to protect her children from an abuser? Or should she stay to protect her children from the disruption of a broken home? One woman described it to me like this: "I did not return to him because I wanted to but because I didn't think it was fair to my children to have to live in the street when they had a warm bed at home."

As a woman tries to figure out how best to care for her children, staying with an abuser may seem to be the more desirable choice. At first glance, this decision makes some sense. If she leaves, she will seriously disrupt the stability of her children's lives. For example, her standard of living—and therefore their standard of living—will drop. Her children may have to move away from their neighborhood. They might have to change schools. They may well lose close friends, a loss that should not be taken lightly. Her husband may have threatened her with a custody battle. She does not want her children exposed to such ugliness. So, in considering her options, a woman may think, "I can put up with it, and he's never actually hit the kids."

The other side to this dilemma is that an abusive home is a terribly toxic environment in which to raise a child. Lundy Bancroft, author of *The Batterer as Parent*, maintains that children in these homes face a variety of threats. There is the threat of being hurt, either accidentally or deliberately. Young children may be injured accidentally, because they are being held by the mother when she is attacked, or simply because they were in the wrong place at the wrong time. Older children may be accidentally hurt when they intervene on their mother's behalf during a violent incident. Some abusers deliberately injure children as a way to punish their partners. (According to Joan Zorza, editor of *Domestic Violence Report* and a strong advocate for children's rights, an abuser is often particularly violent against both the mother and the children when there are children in the home who are not his.) There is also the risk of sexual abuse. Horror stories abound; just open the newspaper.

Not surprisingly, about half of abused women leave when the abuser physically or sexually assaults one of their children. But what mothers do not always realize is that even when children are not physically injured, it is emotionally devastating for a child to witness domestic abuse. Parents often believe that they can hide domestic abuse from their children or that little children are too young to process domestic abuse. The children report differently. Every child in an abusive home knows that there is abuse going on, even if it happens when they are supposed to be asleep, even if it happens in whispers.

Children are also damaged emotionally when abusers use them as a weapon against their mother. The abuser may threaten to take the children from her if she does not behave the way he wants. He may threaten to hurt the children. He may follow through on his threat. He may make them watch as he "punishes" her. He may work to turn the children against her, insisting that they spy on her and report back with an account of what she does when he is away.

You would think that if a woman leaves, her abuser's control over the children would evaporate. She knows better. She knows full well that if she ends the relationship, he will continue to use the children as a way to control her. He may do this through a long, expensive child custody battle. He may threaten to kidnap the children. He may do it. The good news is that most women and children get away safely. But it is important to recognize that concern for her children's safety is a realistic factor that keeps a woman trapped in an abusive relationship.

Abused women are not idiots; they know that a violent home is no place to raise a child. But they often do not understand the full magnitude of what exposure to domestic abuse can do to children. Many women think that if their husbands or boyfriends are not actually hitting the children, and if they occasionally do nice things, like taking them out for ice cream or reading a bedtime story, then they are good fathers. It can take time for a woman to realize that an abuser can *never* be a good father. When mothers realize the damage that is being done to their children, it can mobilize them to escape.

Reason #3: Religion

Religion does not cause abuse. There are certainly religions where men form the sturdy core of the faith and women circle the periphery. I am not here to argue the relative merits of one religion over another. The point is that patriarchal religions do not cause gentle men to turn into abusers. (I've known some mighty sweet patriarchs, including my grandfather, a dear man and an Orthodox rabbi.) What religion *can* do, however, is keep a victim trapped in an abusive marriage.

There is no major religion that condones violence against women. But a religious abuser will deliberately twist and contort doctrine to justify his violence, adding religion to the arsenal of tactics he uses to subdue his victim. "My ex was very knowledgeable in the scriptures when we met," one woman wrote to me, "and I believe that was what attracted me to him in the first place. As time went on and I started to question the scriptures that he would use to 'beat me up' (we all know the ones…wives submit to your husband, etc.), the manipulation and scripture-quoting became worse. At one point he wrote me a four-page letter telling me how I was not being a godly wife and quoted scripture to support his view."

Because the abuser's wife is often religious as well, she is understandably reluctant to resist, since to go against him is to go against her entire religious upbringing. A Mormon woman told me that every Sunday afternoon after church, her husband would force his family to sit in a neat row on their long living room sofa. This was the only time the family was permitted in the living room. As she and the six children sat squeezed together, he would recite passages from the Old and New Testaments "proving" that men were kings in their own households, worthy of being obeyed without question, entitled to mete out punishment for wrongdoing. She was desperately unhappy, of course, but because his subsequent violent acts were always carried out within the context of religious doctrine, punishment for her sins, she felt she had no choice but to submit. It would be easy to trivialize her submission as weakness. I do not. I see a quiet determination, a firm resolve to remain true to her religious values.

Religious abused women often find themselves forced to make desperately difficult trade-offs. For example, if an abused woman is an Orthodox Jew, she will be reluctant to go to a shelter that does not serve kosher food. It's easy enough, perhaps, for an outsider to pooh-

pooh this concern. And the fact is that the laws of Judaism not only permit but actually *require* her to eat nonkosher food under such a circumstance, since the preservation of life takes precedence over all other observances. But that's not the point. The point is that her religion matters to her. Giving up her dietary laws is a violation of her religious values. She ought not to be required to choose between her faith and her personal safety.

Some research indicates that religious women remain in abusive marriages longer than do women who are not religious. "I am a Christian woman," one woman wrote to me. "I believe that religious women stay much longer in abusive marriages because of their commitment to God and not wanting to disappoint God. And we take the duty of a wife and mother very seriously. Not to say that women who are not religious don't; it's just that we are made to feel that we are the glory of our family."

If an abuser in a tight-knit religious community can get the rest of the community behind him, he can damage his victim's credibility to such a degree that it is nearly impossible for her to break free. This was the case for one woman whose mother wrote to me recently. She explained that her daughter "...has a top-notch lawyer because she is up against a very strong Mennonite family who keeps insisting that she CANNOT divorce her husband! They put all the blame on my daughter, saying a man would not act like this if he had a happy home! What we find most amazing is that we live in this small religious community with his family being a huge part of it. Our daughter suffered horribly at the hands of this man and agonized for years how she and her children could get out of this alive. Now, it is all over town; she has had affairs for years and she deserved to be beaten!!!!!! Even her counselor from church said she had to PROVE she was not having an affair. She said statistics point out that a woman does NOT leave a man unless she has someone in the wings! Even the counselor believes my son-in-law's stories. He is GOOD! The show he puts on is spectacular! We take it day to day and pray for help from above to keep her safe and able to protect her children."

These two letters are not unusual; they happen to be from a Christian and a Mennonite, but they could as easily be from any denomination you might name. We would all really like to believe that domestic abuse does not happen to religious people. Or perhaps it happens to *those* people in *that* religion but not to members of *our* religion. Unfortunately, religious leaders are not immune to this sort of thinking.

A religious woman can be greatly influenced by her religious leader. When religious leaders and entire religious communities are silent on the subject of domestic abuse, they are perpetuating the feelings of shame and guilt that haunt victims. Victims are afraid to speak out for fear that they will be misunderstood, rejected, or blamed for their own abuse. "The only way a woman can stand up within my community," a religious Jewish woman wrote to me, "is to be able to go against the entire structure she has lived in since sometimes before she got married, all of her friends she has made, everyone she knows. It is very hard. When you divorce your husband, you divorce your entire community."

It doesn't have to be this way. Outrage is what is needed, outrage toward abusers, and compassion for their victims. When a religious leader condemns a congregant's abusive acts, the entire congregation is strengthened. In many religious communities, enormous changes are underway. Several organizations, most notably The Center for the Prevention of Sexual and Domestic Violence (www.cpsdv.org), have developed materials to teach clergy how to support abused congregants. Seminary students receive training, clergy preach sermons, and there is no doubt in anyone's mind that domestic abuse will not be tolerated. This is a message that religious abused women badly need to hear.

Reason #4: Isolation

Most victims of domestic abuse, whether they realize it or not, are isolated. Being isolated generally does not mean being locked in the attic, though this has been known to happen. Chances are your relative or friend goes to work, walks her children to the school bus, shops for groceries, and even goes to parties. But it would be a mistake to believe that she is not isolated. An abuser works strenuously to drive a wedge between the victim and her family and friends. He does so for one simple reason; these are the very people who would ordinarily step in to protect her.

Isolation is a powerful tactic that allows abusers to achieve enormous control by whittling down the size of their victims' world. Some abusers flat-out forbid their victims to leave the house alone, to visit certain places, or to see certain people. Most abusers are considerably more subtle.

An abuser may keep his victim so busy with tiny tyrannical demands that she finds herself with little opportunity for friendships. She reluctantly drops out of her monthly book club because there seems to be so much to do around the house that she never has a moment free to read the books. She really enjoys her bowling league, but that's the night her husband plays basketball, and he wants to see her in the stands cheering him on. The neighbor she used to meet every day after work for a power walk is put off again and again as the woman rushes to take her husband's shirts to the laundry, pick up his favorite wine, and stop at the butcher for the tiny New Zealand lamb chops he likes. She knows that she could skip these errands, but the evening is so much more pleasant when she doesn't. Gradually, so subtly that she barely remembers when or how it happened, her universe of close personal contacts shrinks down until it contains only one. Him.

Some abusers isolate their victims by chipping away at their credibility. If friends and family members perceive the victims as unreliable at best, unstable at worst, they are reluctant to interfere. An abuser may breathe a word or two about his partner's unfortunate fondness for vodka martinis, murmur a quiet aside about a flirtation that went a bit too far, or whisper a hint about her dwindling supply of sleeping pills. These subtle acts of sabotage are all it takes to establish her as someone whose words should not be taken at face value. "You know Gladys," he'll say with a smile, a wink, or a wry shake of his head. "Not all there, bless her heart, but what are you gonna do?"

Abusers also attempt to isolate their victims from specific people that they find particularly threatening. This may include you! For example, an abuser whose girlfriend has always been close to her older sister may attempt to undermine the friendship. "On the phone with Miss Perfect again?" he sneers. "That bitch never liked me. What kind of ideas was she putting into your head? Don't you think it's time to grow up and make your own decisions?" This puts his partner in a terrible bind. On one hand, she treasures her sister's friendship. On the other hand, her partner is quite right; her sister doesn't like him one little bit! Her boyfriend is difficult to please, but it's not as if she's a battered woman or anything. Perhaps she ought not to speak to her sister so frequently.

Looking at this scenario from the outside, it's easy to see that this man's goal is to drive a wedge between his girlfriend and her sister because her sister is the one person who can help her to see her relationship clearly. For the woman inside the relationship, though, the picture is hazy. The subtle nuances of isolation can be as difficult for an abused woman to fathom as the overall pattern of her abuser's control tactics.

What Else?

As if safety, children, religion, and isolation were not sufficient barriers, there are also the realities of life. Many abused women have serious financial concerns. These concerns affect poor women who must make every dollar do the work of ten. But women of limited means are not the only ones with financial worries. Middle-class and wealthy abusers often use money as a control tactic; their wives have no access to family finances and must humiliatingly beg for everything they need or want. If the abuser agrees that the purchase is worthy, he will give her the money to buy it. If not, she must do without. One woman wrote to me, "I was very disheartened when I realized that the way the system is set up makes help available only to those in less fortunate financial situations. People like me, our lives look good to the world, but in fact we have less because he has control of our entire existence."

Poor women are at serious risk of homelessness if they leave an abuser. Abused professional women face a different problem. These women are isolated in their experience. Each believes she is the only abused woman in her upscale community. Unlike poor women, who are more apt to have used other public services, affluent women are unlikely to seek help from a social worker. If they look for help, it is typically in the private office of a psychologist or marriage counselor. Professional women usually have a great deal to lose by leaving their abusers: an expensive home in a good neighborhood, social standing in the community, private schools for their children. Because so much is riding on their marriages, they may lack supporters, even among their own friends and family.

If a woman has children, she worries how she will feed and house them when she is forced to raise them by herself. "A woman with children is just one man away from the streets," one formerly abused woman told me. She cannot expect support from her abuser; he has probably already made this abundantly clear. She wonders who will look after the children while she is working. Even if they are old enough to attend school during the day, they need a place to go in the afternoon until she can get home. In many communities, her options are limited.

If a woman has not previously worked outside the home, her only health benefits are through her husband's employer. A good job might offer benefits, but she has no assurance that she can find a good job. This is especially true in a rural community or a small town, where employment opportunities can be scarce.

The list of barriers goes on and on—affordable housing, a decent wage, auto insurance, immigration concerns, public transportation.

And then there's love.

"Love is not abuse," I said at the start of this chapter, "and abuse is not love." You might assume that when abuse enters a relationship, love immediately exits. To some extent this is true. However, like much of domestic abuse, it is more complicated than that. Many abused women ultimately stop loving the man who is abusing them, their love eroded by his deliberate attacks on their mind, body, and spirit. It can take substantial time, though. If you want to help a family member or a friend who is being abused, you must never forget that she might still love him. This does not make her a namby-pamby little ninny. After all, every single one of us has been in an intimate relationship with someone. Did we pick someone we hated? Of course not. We picked someone we loved. So did she.

What does an abused woman really want? She wants to have the man she loves, only without all the agony and fear. It can take time— sometimes months, sometimes years—for her to realize that this is not possible. Until that time comes, when she thinks of leaving him, she thinks of leaving the man she thought he would be, the man he used to be, the man he sometimes still is. When she thinks of staying, she thinks of staying with the bastard she knows he can be. It's hard to reconcile these two things.

"For better or worse," the marriage ceremony says. And it says so for a very good reason, because every relationship faces difficulties. If your friend or relative still loves him or once loved him, she will try her best to understand him. "I'm sure part of his hitting and other stuff was his family environment," one woman told me, "because he didn't have a stable family. He saw his mom cheating on his father; he loved his father, and he had to see that. And also his sister killed herself, and he saw a lot of other bad things. I kept trying to rationalize it." Some would call this denial on her part; I do not. I see it as a perfect example of how abusers blame everyone but themselves for their actions. "It's not me," they say. "It's my lousy childhood, my drinking, my boss." The victim's self-talk becomes, "If I can be strong, if I can weather the storm, if I can just love him enough, then I can turn him around." In other words, if she can hang in there when things are worse, they will eventually get better.

Right—and chickens have lips. But it would be a serious mistake to dismiss her love as stupidity, weakness, or stunning lack of insight. Instead, see it for what it is: the fierce determination to do whatever it takes to make this relationship work. You cannot argue her out of her love. It is something she must arrive at on her own, and she probably will. Most women do stop loving the man who is abusing them. One woman wrote to me, "I miss him sometimes but I realize that I only miss the man I wanted him to be."

Is Leaving Her Only Option?

So far, we've been discussing the barriers that keep an abused woman from leaving her abuser, as if leaving is her only option. This raises an interesting question. Must she leave? Or, is there a way that she can stay? This may be a question you have pondered as you try to help your friend or relative think through her options. You may be a firm believer in marriage as a lifelong commitment. You may be deeply distressed at the high rate of divorce in our country. Surely, you think to yourself, ending a marriage should be the last possible resort. a drastic measure contemplated only when all others have failed. Surely, even an abusive relationship can get better.

Theoretically, this is true, but only under one condition. For an abusive relationship to change, the *abuser* has to change. He has to take full responsibility for his actions. He has to want to change. And he has to do something about it; he has to undertake the long, hard process of changing not only his behavior but the core values and beliefs underlying that behavior. (More about this in Chapter 4.) If an abuser does these things, there is a possibility he may change. And if he is able to change, then there is a possibility that the relationship can change for the better.

If, however, her abuser refuses to hold himself accountable for his actions, then all bets are off. The physical abuse may diminish or even stop completely, but the relationship itself will never be peaceful. In that case, your friend or relative's best chance is to escape from the relationship.

The Balance Tips

With all the barriers abused women face, it is a wonder they ever manage to escape. But they do all the time. I have been privileged to meet many women who escaped from abusive husbands or boyfriends. What I have learned from these women is that breaking free of domestic abuse is never a single act; it is a process. At some point the balance tips. Leaving becomes preferable to staying.

There is a shift at some point from fear and sadness to anger and contempt. Until that shift occurs, leaving is unlikely. It may even be undesirable. Why do I say it's undesirable? If a woman is being abused and her abuser refuses to change his behavior, isn't it always best for her to leave him? Not necessarily. If she attempts to escape without a safety plan, adequate childcare, financial resources, affordable housing, legal protection, and a strong support system, she may very well go back. Or even worse, she and her children might be seriously injured or killed.

Generally, leaving slowly with a plan is safer and more successful than running out the door in a panic. The women who get away safely, the women who don't go back, are the ones who have already grown strong inside. If your friend or family member is being abused, you can be helpful by understanding how her abuser's relentless campaign of domestic abuse has weakened her, by realizing that there are many perfectly legitimate reasons why she stays, and by standing beside her as she works to become strong again.

Understanding Psychological Abuse

If She Isn't Being Hit, Is It Really Abuse?

When people think of domestic abuse, they generally think of physical violence. If their family member or friend isn't being punched in the nose, then her relationship may be pretty crummy, but it isn't abusive. As you are beginning to realize, this is not so. For one thing, there are many ways to be physically abused that do not leave visible scars. For another, domestic abuse is never a single incident; it is a campaign to achieve control. Abusers use an assortment of tactics to control their victims, many of which are not physical.

Last year, on the second floor of Nordstrom's, I spotted a couple in their mid-30s. The stunningly attractive woman was trying on jeans, while the man sat in a chair so close to the fitting room entryway that he seemed to be guarding it. The woman emerged at intervals from a booth, modeling this pair and that, ostensibly looking in the mirror but in fact waiting for his judgment. He had her walk, turn, pose, and then he delivered the verdict. "That pair is too short. Try another." "I think the first ones fit you better at the waist."

There was nothing overtly negative about their interaction. But he never asked her what she liked. He never asked if the jeans felt comfortable, something only she would know. She listened quietly, neither agreeing nor disagreeing. The saleswoman popped into the woman's booth occasionally to pick up the rejects but interacted only with her companion. "How did that pair work for her?" she asked. "Do you want me to bring it in a different size?"

What was going on here? The fact is, there's no way for any of us to know. The guy might be a teeny bit anal about clothing, and she cuts him a little slack because you have to pick your battles. Or the scene in the dressing room may have been a brief peek into this woman's nightmare world of domestic abuse. Or the two of them might be a perfectly ordinary couple. He doesn't control how she dresses, whom she sees, where she goes, and what she does with her time. He doesn't comment on every outfit she wears, every meal she cooks, and every book she reads. She doesn't tiptoe through the day, trying to get it right. She simply likes to have him along when she goes shopping.

What Is Psychological Abuse?

Psychological abuse is tricky. It is difficult for your friend or relative to comprehend, and it is equally difficult for you to comprehend. It is far murkier than the punches, slaps, rapes, and gunshots of physical violence. Many people use the terms verbal or emotional abuse to describe the toxic mix of insults, unreasonable demands, blaming, threats, financial control, jealousy, and other daily degradations that an abuser uses to diminish, dominate, and control his wife or girlfriend. I stay away from these two terms because I find them trivializing. Verbal abuse sounds like somebody yelled. Emotional abuse sounds like somebody cried. And let's face it; even in the best of relationships, someone is going to yell and someone is going to cry!

I prefer the term psychological abuse because it captures the motivation of the abuser. Psychological abuse is not an angry word or even a whole bunch of angry words. It is an *intentional, deliberate attempt to cause mental suffering*. The abuser's motivation is to achieve control now and in the future. Some abusers are able to maintain control of the relationship with psychological abuse alone. Others use a combination of physical and psychological abuse.

Because psychological abuse is not as easy to pin down as physical abuse, it can be both over-diagnosed and under-diagnosed. I worry, for example, when I hear a caller to a radio talk show describe her boyfriend as psychologically abusive when what she actually means is that they had a fight the previous night. There are nasty, cruel, mean people in this world; I try to avoid them whenever possible. But it would be a mistake to call these people abusers. A psychological abuser is more than just a no-goodnik. His abuse is considered, determined, and precisely targeted to his victim's weaknesses. I am not saying that victims of domestic abuse are weak—far from it. We all have zones of weakness, zones that that can be penetrated if someone chooses to do so. A porcupine's quills protect it from forest predators. But an especially canny predator will dart in close and flip the porcupine onto its back, knowing that the absence of quills on its soft belly leaves it open to attack.

It's Not Just Yelling

Yelling

Several years ago, my home state of Utah released a domestic violence report based on a random telephone survey of households in cities, small towns, and rural communities. To the surprise and shock of all but those of us who already knew, Utah's figures were identical to the rest of the country. There was no more domestic violence here than elsewhere—and no less. A local broadcaster delivered the numbers on the evening news. "Thirty-four percent of the households reported verbal abuse," he solemnly intoned, "which I guess means yelling." Sigh. I do wish newscasters would check their facts before they read the news. Psychological abuse is far more than yelling, though some abusers do indeed yell.

Do not underestimate the power of yelling. Being yelled at is never pleasant. But when an abuser yells, rages, bellows, shouts, howls, or otherwise makes an outcry, he can be downright scary. One woman described it to me like this: "It's like living with a wild animal. Some wild animals are beautiful, but this is somebody who is not. He's ugly to me when he yells. It's like being in a room with a beast." Yelling is a powerful control tactic because it keeps an abuser's victim under his thumb while leaving no evidence. If the neighbors hear loud shouts and call the police, the detectives can do little unless the abuser destroyed property or injured the victim.

Threats

Threats of physical violence are another powerful psychological tactic that abusers use to keep their victims in line. "Going to the mall with your mother again?" a man might ask his girlfriend, the warning tone in his voice belying his tiny smile. "You'd better watch what you spend, honeybunch. I may have to punish you." Based on prior experience, she knows that he will unpack her shopping bags and scrutinize each sales slip, despite the fact that she has her own credit cards and has never in her life made a late payment. He may simply keep her awake all night, scolding her for her irresponsible spending habits, or he may take off his wide leather belt and beat her "for her own good." So she tucks her purchases in the trunk of her mother's car, making a feeble excuse that she and her mom both know is pure nonsense.

Words

Then there are words. "Cucumber nose," a man called his wife until she could practically see her nose growing each time she looked in her bathroom mirror. In desperation, she sought the services of a cosmetic surgeon. There is more to the story; a few days after surgery, as she lay on her back recuperating, he swung his arm across the bed and hit her nose with his forearm. Accidentally, he said. You can imagine the pain. But that's beside the point. The crux of her story is not the physical attack on her nose but the psychological one on her as a person.

A teenager in Akron, Ohio, put it brilliantly. When I make presentations to teens, I have them write their questions on index cards. One card read, "If a man continually tells a woman how fat and ugly she is, why would he want to be with her?" That's really the issue, isn't it? If this woman's husband found her nose so repulsive, why the heck did he marry her? The answer, of course, is that the length of her nose did not bother *him*—it bothered *her*. And he knew it. So he tortured her with it.

Never underestimate the destructiveness of words. "I am very intelligent," one woman wrote to me. "I speak four languages well, and also speak Cantonese, which I learned in Hong Kong. He told me on several occasions that I was stupid to learn Cantonese instead of Mandarin." Excuse me? Stupid to learn *Cantonese*? What was going on here? I don't know this for a fact, but I strongly suspect that this woman's husband, a wealthy American businessman, knew far fewer languages than she did. A nonabusive man would have been delighted with her accomplishment, proud that while he was out making heaps of money, his wife was not confined to the American sector in Hong Kong but could instead mingle easily in this international community. Her abusive husband found her fluency threatening. So he belittled her for learning the "wrong" dialect, Cantonese instead of Mandarin. I don't know about you, but I can't speak either one.

Used with precision, an abuser's words make his victim feel uncertain of herself and, therefore, easier to control. Most of us would feel pretty proud of ourselves for mastering Cantonese. But this woman was not permitted to take pleasure in her achievement. Her husband had to minimize, trivialize, and ridicule her accomplishment and, by implication, her. If he could make her feel stupid, then he could feel smart. If he could make her feel weak, then he could feel strong. If he could convince her that she couldn't make it without him, then she'd never leave him. She did, though, a few years later. She finally saw through all his baloney. That's the irony of domestic abuse. It works, but only up to a point.

The Look

And then there's The Look. Some abusers have become so skilled at maintaining control over their victims that they can do it without words. If a man has been physically violent once, he is capable of doing it again. His victim realizes this. When he looks at her in a particular way, she knows that she had better shape up. "I called it The Bull," one woman told me. "It was like his nostrils would start flaring and he'd start getting that look in his eyes and he'd start pacing. It was just like a bull, you know. Just a bull that's ready to charge." Terrifying, and the more terrifying for being silent.

There is another version of The Look. One woman called her husband's look "The Frozen Tundra," his cold lack of emotion transforming her into a nonperson. It was as though he was saying, "You mean no more to me than the table, the refrigerator, or the vacuum cleaner." Objectifying. Dismissive.

He Never Hit Me

The woman whose husband ridiculed her mastery of Cantonese did not think of herself as a victim of domestic violence. She described her husband not as a violent man but as a control freak. She wrote, "At home, he was an absolute control freak. Shortly after we moved into a 10-million-dollar home in Hong Kong, he went ballistic because the soap in the bathroom didn't match the room." Okay, I thought to myself when I read her letter, her husband controlled her with psychological tactics. These tactics worked so he didn't have to resort to physical violence. Then I read her next paragraph. "There was very little physical abuse," it began, "except one time in Hong Kong when he tried to strangle me." Yikes!

If you want to understand psychological abuse, it is important to realize that it frequently is accompanied by a certain amount of physical abuse—not a broken leg, not a knife wound, not a trip in an ambulance to the emergency room, but physical abuse nevertheless. Your family member or friend may tell you that she is "only" being psychologically abused. Like the woman in Hong Kong, she may well believe it. If you listen carefully, you may discover that her husband or boyfriend also uses physical intimidation and occasional physical violence to keep her in line.

I heard the following story from a divorced woman who lived in a small town on the Florida coast. "He never hit me," she insisted. "If he had hit me, I would have left." So I asked her to tell me about a time that was really upsetting, and this is what she told me. One night she and her husband were having an argument that started over dinner, continued through the evening, and escalated when they got into bed. Because she was in bed, she was wearing only a light nightgown. He yanked her out of bed, dragged her downstairs, pushed her out the front door, and locked the door behind her. When she banged on the door, pleading to be let back into the house, he said, "I'm doing this for your own good. You're out of control. You're a crazy woman. I'm going back to bed; I'll unlock the door in the morning when you've come to your senses."

It was winter. She was barefoot. She could have walked to a neighbor's house, but she was barely dressed. Besides, she was mortified. Ultimately, though, she was so cold she felt she had no choice. So she summoned up her courage and walked to the neighboring house, ringing their bell at two o'clock in the morning. The neighbors let her in and made up a bed for her on the sofa, but it was clear that they were uncomfortable being pulled into a private squabble between hus-band and wife.

When the woman returned to her house at six o'clock the follow-ing morning, the front door was unlocked. Her husband blandly insisted that he had no idea what she was talking about; the door had been unlocked all night. He supposed she had simply been so hyster-ical that she was unable to work the doorknob.

You may be wondering what you would have done if you had been that woman. So did I. We would all like to think that we would have packed our bags and walked out, making darned sure that we locked the door behind us! But I can't honestly say that's what I would have done. I think I might very well have begun to doubt myself. Maybe I *had* been hysterical. I certainly was crying as I was being dragged downstairs. Perhaps the door wasn't really locked. If it wasn't and I had made a big fuss over nothing and involved the neighbors, I'd feel pretty stupid. I would just want to put the whole sorry episode out of my mind as soon as possible. Eventually, I would probably have left the marriage. Many women do leave. And I would have said—and truly believed—that my ex-husband was *psychologically* abusive but never *physically* abusive. Looking at this woman's story from the out-side, I think you would agree that her husband's abuse was a combi-nation of both.

The "Uh-Oh" Feeling

Psychological abuse hurts. It hurts badly. Even abused women who have suffered severe physical assaults report that the psychological abuse and degradation are more difficult to bear. One woman explained it to me like this: "I would take the physical abuse any day over the emotional abuse. The emotional abuse is far worse. I mean, as far as physical abuse goes, the pain and bruises go away, but the emotional abuse, it never goes away. Even going to a psychologist, it helps you get over it and go on, but it never goes away; it just never goes away."

How can you tell if your family member or friend is being psycho-logically abused? Trust your instincts. Trust the uh-oh feeling you get in the pit of your stomach when you are with the two of them. Perhaps he is a real charmer but you find his charm a little off. Maybe he makes a few too many jokes at her expense, passing them off as nothing more than harmless teasing. He gripes about the amount of money she spends on clothes. He flirts at parties but gets annoyed if she does the same. She used to entertain friends with long and amusing stories; now she lets him do all the talking. Whenever she does speak, she sneaks a look at him afterwards as if to gauge his reaction.

Psychological abuse is an intentional attempt to get inside the victim's head and learn to use her zones of weakness against her. It can be far more destructive than physical abuse because of its very invisibility. A victim of psychological abuse does not see a black eye in her mirror, clear evidence that someone attacked her. Your family member or friend may not see the subtle signs of her abuser's psychological tactics or understand that she is being deliberately undermined. You can be helpful by understanding that an abuser uses what he learns about her weak zones in a considered, deliberate way to cause her mental suffering. You can realize that, although physical abuse can take a life, psychological abuse can destroy a spirit.

Understanding Abusers

Would You Know an Abuser if You Saw One?

I recently participated in a community's Domestic Violence Awareness Weekend. The planning committee had decided, quite rightly, to include teenagers as well as their parents. While the adults sat politely in the community center auditorium and listened to my standard "Domestic Violence 101" lecture, the teens gathered in the gymnasium for an afternoon of noisy learning. Later, they marched in to show us grownups what they had accomplished. One of their assignments had been to create a television ad about dating violence. A small group assembled on the stage and, with nervous giggles, took their places.

Imagine it. Enter stage left a girl striding down an imaginary sidewalk. Following a few feet behind her on tiptoe, a tall boy wearing a furry black fright wig. The Stalker. Mr. Bad Guy. His fingers curve like claws as he lifts his arms to grab her. "Rarrr!" he growls. She whirls, whips a small can of hair spray from her jacket pocket, and points it at him with a loud "Pssst!" Her would-be attacker drops to the ground, kicks his legs a few times, and finally lies still. The rest of the group sings the jingle. "Pepper spray! Pepper spray! Spraaaaay the violence awaaaaay!"

We all clapped enthusiastically. It was a cute skit, downright adorable. But it will not keep a single one of these kids safe from domestic abuse, because most abusers don't go "rarrr."

Actually, that's not strictly true. Some abusers *do* go "rarrr." These abusers are pretty easy to spot; I think of them as the bar fight guys. If your family member or friend is involved with a man like this, then you (and everyone else in your community) know all about him. He may get into fights, he may have been involved in road-rage incidents, he may have been brought up on assault charges, and he may even have served jail time. Or his anger may show itself in less obvious ways. For example, his belligerence toward employers and coworkers may have gotten him fired. "I never get a fair shake," he whines, as yet another fed up boss sends him packing. The family may move frequently, as arguments with neighbors escalate out of control. "The people in this town are narrow-minded bigots," he grouses while he packs the car. This type of abuser does not specifically target his family. When violence flares at home, it's just business as usual.

Most abusers, though, are only violent in the privacy of their own homes. They get along well with friends and neighbors. They hold a steady job. They are respected in their social or religious communities. This type of abuser does not have an anger management problem. He is able to manage his anger perfectly well under most circumstances. When he is cut off in traffic, his response may be limited to a few salty words mumbled discreetly under his breath. If his secretary is prone to typos, he may fire her, but he won't punch her in the nose. His neighbor's dog may have an unfortunate tendency to piddle on his prize roses, but he does not respond by strangling her or her dog.

When this type of abuser is physically or psychologically abusive toward his wife or girlfriend, he is often *well* under control. For example, he waits until he is alone, away from witnesses. He delivers stomach punches, so there will be no obvious bruises. He threatens, which leaves no scars. One woman told me that her husband would drive recklessly, then minimize it afterwards. As she sat in the passenger seat, teary-eyed and shaken, he would calmly explain that she that she was exaggerating, that she was hysterical, that it hadn't been a big deal. This is not someone out of control; after all, they never did get into an accident. He knew how to drive just wildly enough to terrify her without losing control of the car.

Who ARE These Guys?

Given the right combination of circumstances, I might commit a violent act. So might you. People become violent for any number of reasons: to protect themselves or others, to right a wrong, to achieve monetary gain, or to control the behavior of others. The question is, why do abusers commit violent acts? In other words, who ARE these guys?

There are many misunderstandings about abusive men. One is that domestic abuse is caused by DTP, deadly testosterone poisoning. In other words, men are simply prone to violence. Are they? It is certainly true that most abusers are men, but it is not equally true that most men are abusers. This is not a war of the hormones, an inevitable biological clash between estrogen and testosterone. If it were, then there would be more of it; every heterosexual relationship would be abusive. And there would be no domestic abuse in gay or lesbian relationships.

Another misunderstanding is that abusive men simply reflect the violence around them. Children today are exposed to a shocking degree of violence. Movies, television, popular song lyrics, Internet sites, and video games contain words and images that make my toes curl. No matter how hard a parent tries, it is impossible to protect children from these influences. But that's precisely the point; *all* children are exposed. If abusers sprang fully formed from the violent culture around them, then two boys who live next door to each other, play on the same football team, watch the same movies, and visit the same Internet sites will both grow up to be abusers. And that simply does not happen.

Some people believe that men from certain countries or ethnic groups are more abusive than men from the United States. During my guest lecture at a medical school in St. Louis, a third-year medical student reported that he had asked his supervisor how to effectively support clinic patients he knew were being beaten but who denied it. The supervisor, the student told me, had replied, "Don't waste your time. It's what they're used to. In their country, all the men beat up their women. It's a cultural thing." I have also had family members of victims tell me, "Our sister is married to a man from one of those ethnic groups where domestic violence is considered acceptable. That's why he beats her up." Nonsense. While abuse *tactics* can vary from culture to culture, women are abused in nearly all modern countries and cultures. There are more similarities among abusers than there are differences. During a lecture tour in Texas, I asked Irina, a recent immigrant from Uzbekistan, whether she believes there is such a thing as Russian domestic violence. Her reply was swift and sure. "There's no such thing. Pain is pain."

In some countries, certainly, women have fewer rights. As a result, the *punishment* of domestic violence might be less harsh in these countries than in the United States; the abuser may not even be punished at all. Even so, it would be a mistake to think that abusers only come from countries where women's rights are limited. For one thing, countries on every continent now have laws that prohibit domestic violence. To a certain extent, pointing our fingers at other countries is a way to ignore the problems in our own country. The abuse of women, and society's tolerance for such abuse, is a big problem throughout the world. If your friend or relative is being abused by a man who hails from another country, don't make the mistake of believing that his heritage is causing his abuse. He's doing it all on his own. Besides, it doesn't matter where he may have been born. If he currently resides in the United States, or in many other countries around the world, he is living in a country where domestic violence is illegal.

Then there are sports heroes. When a professional athlete is arrested for beating his wife, the story makes the front page of the sports section. Do all the highly competitive and aggressive men who dominate the world of sports bring this belligerence home with them? Does a man who is accustomed to stomping on a quarterback feel it is his God-given right to stomp on his wife?

Sometimes he does. I keep a file of stories about professional athletes. I find their excuses fascinating, since these abusers in particular are so much bigger and stronger than their victims. One pro football player described the night of his arrest. His wife was driving the car. He claimed that *he* was the victim; as she drove, she hit him with her fists and her cell phone. "She was beating on me," he said, "and I put my hands up to ward off the blows from her hands and from a phone. And in the process of doing that, *her lip got split*, either from the cell phone bouncing back or whatever. It certainly wasn't me, because I have never struck a woman." (My husband and I tried this. I sat in the driver's seat of my car, Neal sat in the passenger's seat, and I pretended to flail at him with my cell phone. He put his arm up to protect his face. Sure enough, my phone bounced off his arm! But it didn't go anywhere near my lip. And, as you have probably guessed, my lip certainly did not get split.)

Although some athletes do beat their wives or girlfriends, most athletes are aggressive only where they are paid to be aggressive: on the football field, the basketball court, or the hockey rink. Even there, when they are overly feisty, they are penalized. Referees run out and wave little flags, and the offender loses whatever advantage he gained. I probably haven't described this correctly—sports are not my strong suit—but I'm sure you get my point. It would be a mistake to think that an abuser can only be a testosterone-poisoned, Internet-surfing, football-playing hunk. Some abusers play chess. Some have season tickets to the ballet.

So who ARE these guys? What's going on in the mind of an abuser? Lundy Bancroft is considered one of the world's experts on the behavior of abusive men. In his book *Why Does He DO That?* Bancroft writes, "Abuse grows from attitudes and values, not feelings. The roots are ownership, the trunk is entitlement, and the branches are control. Abusers are far more conscious of what they are doing than they appear to be. However, even their less-conscious behaviors are driven by their core attitudes." Bancroft devotes an entire chapter to the abusive mentality, identifying 10 core attitudes of abusers. I present a summary of his list here in the hope that it will help you get a handle on the mindset of the person who is hurting someone you care about.

1. He is controlling.
2. He feels entitled.
3. He twists things into their opposites.
4. He disrespects his partner and considers himself superior to her.
5. He confuses love and abuse.
6. He is manipulative.
7. He strives to have a good public image.
8. He feels justified.
9. He denies and minimizes his abuse.
10. He is possessive.

Abusers are still a puzzle. Although Bancroft's list of abuser attitudes is useful, it still does not address the key question: What makes them tick? I believe that we do not fully understand and may never know the answer. Is it society, cultural messages, genes, a psychological flaw? I don't find any of these explanations completely satisfactory. It may be that abuse arises from a potent brew of many causes. Or different abusers may have different causes, since there are probably diverse types of abusers, just as there are diverse types of cancers, it may be that we will never find one over-arching explanation. All science is slow, which means we must act as best we can, hoping we are correct.

In a way, though, the cause does not matter much. It *would* matter if we could be proactive about domestic violence, stopping it before it starts. Wouldn't that be lovely! Find the at-risk boys and gently steer them in another direction before they grow into abusive men. Perhaps some day we will learn how to accomplish this with abusers, embezzlers, child molesters, and others. Until that time, the *cause* of abusive behavior isn't all that important. The *effect* is what matters, an abuser's core attitudes of ownership, entitlement, and control.

What Are Abusers Like as Fathers?

To the outside world, to people who do not understand what an abusive relationship is like, it may seem that an abuser is a perfectly splendid father. "I've never seen him yell at the kids," family members may claim. "And he certainly doesn't hit them." Now that you have a sense of what abusers are like to their wives or girlfriends, you can probably guess what they are like as fathers. Your instinct probably tells you that no abuser is capable of being a fully responsible parent.

Abusers may be rigid and authoritarian fathers. They expect to be obeyed instantly and will not tolerate any resistance or arguing from their children. I haven't met any children over the age of two who calmly accept every parental directive without question. Wise parents tolerate, perhaps even encourage, a certain amount of healthy debate. But when abusers say "Jump!" the only response they want to hear is "How high?" Many abusers swing unpredictably between authoritarian and permissive parenting, or between authoritarian parenting and total lack of interest in their children.

Some abusers show a remarkable lack of affection toward their children most of the time. Then, on rare occasions, they turn into the good daddy; joking, playing games, and spending money freely. Absence, they say, makes the heart grow fonder. This lack of availability, interspersed now and then with attention, increases their value in their children's eyes.

Finally, an abuser may be self-centered. Everything in the house revolves around daddy. He expects his children to meet his needs rather than the other way around. These are families where any noise or playing in the house has to stop if daddy is feeling tired or irritable. Family members must pay attention to his minor successes or failures. Children learn that they had better be affectionate with their father, whether they want to or not. When any of these needs are not met to daddy's satisfaction, he will make life miserable for everyone around him.

Is It Her Fault?

It is dreadful to believe that the world is a random place, that we are safe only by chance or luck. This is why an airplane crash is more frightening than a car crash and why a house destroyed by a tornado is more frightening than that same house destroyed by fire. When we look for common characteristics of women who are injured by a husband or boyfriend, we are really saying, "I need to find the ways in which they are not like me. Then I won't have to worry that I (or my daughter, or my sister, or my best friend) would ever experience such a thing." Abused women have only one characteristic in common; they are all female. This is not what people want to hear. They want to hear that abused women are poor, or uneducated, or drug users, or from violent homes. Some are; others are not. This makes people twitch.

Even if people accept that a victim's educational level, ethnicity, or childhood might be just like theirs, they still wonder if her abuser's behavior is somehow her fault. "My husband is a cardiologist," the Akron woman who approached me after my presentation told me. "His latest excuse, that he started this week, is that he treats me this way because I piss him off. If I wouldn't piss him off, he wouldn't treat me this way." Many people wonder if an abuser is simply an ordinary fellow who is pissed off because his wife or girlfriend is a real—excuse me—bitch. This is because most people are not abusers. In the past, when you heard about a man beating up his wife or girlfriend, you may have thought, "I don't get it. I could *never* imagine hurting the person I love. What on earth could make someone do that?" Perhaps you concluded that you would have to be seriously provoked. Only if she were horrible, only if she were a truly ghastly human being, only if she really pushed your buttons, would you become so angry that you would lose control and become violent.

Oddly enough, this is the same argument that abusers make! Whenever abusers are asked why they beat up their wives or girl-friends, they are always eager to explain. But their explanations always center on something *their victims* did! She served pizza for dinner three nights in a row. She didn't change the baby's dirty diaper. She brought home the wrong brand of cigarettes from the convenience store.

I know…I know…these sound pretty trivial. But sometimes the victim has done something that would make *anyone* angry. She had an affair. She ran up a gargantuan credit card debt. She smashed the family car into a tree while driving drunk. She may be an appalling individual. That's irrelevant. Most men *do not* beat their wives or girlfriends, no matter how angry they become. A man may become downright livid with his wife or girlfriend. Over time, his love may turn to weary disgust until eventually he ends the relationship. But he will not become abusive for the simple reason that he is not an abuser. As my father's oldest friend Lou said in a recent phone call, "I know that a relationship might deteriorate over time. But how could a man hit someone he once loved?" My husband Neal weighed in with his own question: "Everyone always asks why an abused woman doesn't just leave. But if she is supposedly so horrible to live with that she drives a man to violence, why doesn't *he* just leave?" Good point.

An abuser always tells his victim that she is responsible for the abuse. She may also get this message from others. The gist of the message is, "It takes two to tango. What did *you* do to make him so mad?" You may have said something like this to your friend or relative as you struggled to come to terms with her situation. The sad part is that, after awhile, the victim starts to believe that it *is* all her fault; she started it, and she is responsible for stopping it. Abused women spend a lot of time and energy trying to second-guess their abusers. This is an exhausting job, because what is right one day is wrong the next. The soup that was dismissed yesterday for being too salty will be angrily rejected today for not being salty enough.

If you want to help your family member or friend, it is critical to realize that *her actions* have nothing to do with *his behavior.* Ultimately, abuse is a choice that he has made. An abuser always claims that his victim caused his abuse; that if she had not nagged him, questioned him about money, refused to have sex with him and so on, he would not have been forced to punish her. And perhaps she *does* do all these things…and worse. But most men *do not* abuse their wives or girlfriends, no matter what they may have done. A nonabusive man may well end the relationship. An abuser typically will not.

What About Alcohol and Drugs?

The link between substance abuse and domestic violence is a complicated one. If the person who is abusing your friend or family member also drinks heavily or takes drugs, it is important for you to understand how these two problems are related. The link is not as clear-cut as you might think.

At first glance, it would seem to make sense that domestic violence is caused by substance abuse and that ending one will end the other. After all, we know people get into serious car accidents when they are under the influence of drugs or alcohol. So it's understandable to imagine that domestic violence works the same way. Victims and those who care about them find it easier to attribute domestic violence to alcohol and drugs because these are outside the abuser. An abused woman comforts herself with the notion that he doesn't really mean to hit her— it's just the booze or the pills. If he could only get sober, she reasons, then he'd be a good man. This is a happier thought than the possibility that he *does* mean it.

The victim is not the only one who blames the abuse on his drug problem. He does it, too. Abusers frequently blame their drinking or drug use for their violence and claim they cannot help themselves. This sounds good, but it isn't true. The truth is, many people drink or use drugs. Only some abuse their partners.

Although there is certainly a connection between substance abuse and domestic violence, there is no evidence that substance abuse *causes* domestic violence. For example, abusive men with severe alcohol problems are just as likely to abuse their partners when they are sober as when they are drunk. Some, in fact, commit their worst abuse when they are sober. Others deliberately get drunk so they can justify their violence. In other words, *he does not beat her because he drinks; he drinks in order to beat her.* The reality is that most men who drink alcohol do not become violent or aggressive. And there are many abusers who drink only lemonade and swallow nothing stronger than aspirin.

Although substance abuse does not cause domestic violence, it *can* increase a victim's risk of injury or death. An abusive man who is also a substance abuser may be more violent and cause greater injury that an abuser who is not. An abuser who drinks or takes drugs may lose control of his judgment or coordination. For example, his usual way to attack his partner might be to push her against a wall. If he has been drinking, however, he may lose his balance and push her down a flight of stairs. He may usually strangle her until she loses consciousness. Under the influence of drugs, he may misjudge and kill her. Amphetamines heighten excitability and paranoia. They may lead to impulsive acts. Abusers who use large quantities of amphetamines, and who already have aggressive personalities, are likely to become more impulsive when they use amphetamines.

Most experts agree that stopping the alcohol or drug use does not stop the violence. In other words, if an abuser enters a drug rehab program, that's nice, but he needs to be treated separately for his abusiveness. This is because the underlying philosophy of batterer intervention programs and 12-step programs such as Alcoholics Anonymous (AA) are different. For example, AA programs treat alcoholism as a *disease.* They teach that the alcoholic's partner is codependent. They emphasize the importance of family therapy to help the alcoholic recover. Batterer treatment programs treat violence as a *choice.* They teach that the batterer's partner is never responsible for the abuser's actions but is forced into a state of submission by the abuser's threats and actions. They recommend against family therapy since it is not safe for the victim.

Although substance abuse treatment will not end domestic abuse, it may be possible for an abuser to attend both programs at the same time because there are some similarities between them. Both break through barriers such as rationalizing, denial, blaming others, and minimizing. Both emphasize the importance of taking personal responsibility for behavior. Both emphasize that personal change must occur over the long term.

Unfortunately, there is no evidence that conquering substance abuse results in decreased domestic abuse. Abused women with substance-abusing partners often report that during recovery the domestic abuse continues and often escalates. "At least when he got drunk enough, he'd pass out," one woman told me. "Not that I'd want him back on the booze, you know. But now the kids and I don't ever get a break from him. It's like he blames us for having to get sober, so we're the ones who have to pay." Even when the physical abuse decreases, the psychological abuse, such as threats, manipulation, jealousy, and isolation, can get worse once the perpetrator becomes sober.

Can He Change?

Many victims of domestic abuse hang in there, hoping against hope that their husbands or boyfriends will change. Abusers learn to feed this hope. Many abusers, faced with the possibility of losing their partners, will make extravagant promises to change, only to return to their abusive behavior once they have been forgiven.

Is change possible? To answer this question, we have to remind ourselves of what motivates an abuser. In most cases, he is not a man with a hot temper who simply needs to learn how to manage his anger. This is a man who needs 100 percent of the control in a relationship 100 percent of the time. He is a man who achieves this control by mounting a campaign against his wife or girlfriend, using a combination of psychological and physical tactics.

In order to change, he would have to do something extraordinarily uncomfortable and difficult:; he would have to decide that *his need for control is less important than his need for a loving, intimate relationship with his family*. Then he would have to undergo the long and painful process of examining his behavior, taking responsibility for his actions, and learning how to function as an equal partner in his intimate relationship.

In order to change, he would have to drop the excuses. You already understand one common abuser excuse; he blames his wife or girlfriend for his own actions. She spent too much money. She flirted with his best friend. She wore too much makeup, or not enough. Abusers also minimize their abuse. They use words that trivialize their assaults: a smack, a tap, or a poke. "I shmushed her face a little," a man explains earnestly. The victim's broken jaw attests to an attack far more vicious than a "shmush." Some abusers flat-out deny their actions, wondering aloud how on earth their victims managed to acquire that ugly purple bruise on her shoulder. Others justify their abuse by pointing to some outside force. "It only happened because I was under a lot of pressure at work. I just walked in the front door, I wanted my dinner, and already she was in my face about stuff," he may say. "She should have known to stay out of my way when I got home from work." Next time, this man's indignant justification might be that it was Sunday afternoon and he was watching the football game.

Is change possible? I am an unabashed optimist. I still believe that Cinderella's fairy godmother went "poof!" and the pumpkin turned into a Lexus. But, although I think most of us are theoretically capable of change, I do realize that such change typically requires more than a well-placed poof. In order to change, we have to acknowledge that we have a problem. For example, some people are alcoholics. They decide to stop drinking and, either by themselves or with the help of a support group like AA, they stop. But the key is that they acknowledge *they* are the ones who must do the changing.

So what would it take for an abuser to change? It would take saying, "I am an abuser, and I want to stop." This could happen in the person's first relationship, or in his fifth, but at some point in life, this person would have to wake up and say, "I keep messing up. Women keep leaving me. I finally get it. My sense of entitlement, my belief that I own my wife or girlfriend, my need to control my intimate partner, is keeping me from having a loving relationship." The person could work on this alone, or he could get professional help. I honestly don't know how many abusers get this kind of wake-up call; my experience and my instincts tell me that it does not happen often. An abuser spends all his energy convincing his victim that the abuse is her fault, that if only she was prettier, if only the house was cleaner, if only the children were better behaved, then he would treat her well. An abuser would have to get past all that and realize that *he* is the one with the problem before change would even be a possibility.

Okay, you may be wondering, but what about batterer treatment programs? Aren't they supposed to help men stop their violent behavior? Yes, they are. To a certain extent, for certain abusers, these programs are effective; they are, at the very least, the best we have to offer at this time. They send a message that violence is not okay, they hold batterers accountable for their actions, and they offer the possibility of change. But the men in batterer treatment programs are not there because they accept that they have a problem. They are in these programs because a judge said "batterer treatment or jail," and—no surprise—they chose batterer treatment.

I have great respect for the people who run batterer programs. Although statistics vary from program to program, my colleagues who lead or direct these programs tell me that only about one batterer in five reaches the point where he acknowledges his own responsibility for his violent behavior. Even this small subset aren't then magically cured; they still have a long way to go. But at least for these men, change is theoretically possible.

For some victims, simply decreasing the threat of serious harm is good enough, at least for the time being. Once a battered woman feels physically safe, once she can stop worrying about getting killed, she can take the time to plan for her future. This is one major benefit of batterer treatment programs; they give the batterer's victim a little breathing space. Breathing space, though, is not the same as peace. In the book *Why Does He DO That?* Lundy Bancroft identifies words and actions that, in his professional experience, would demonstrate that an abuser has changed not only his abusive acts but the values and thinking underlying those acts. I have summarized these in Checklist 3. I leave it to you to decide if the man who has been abusing your friend or relative will choose to make such deep and long-lasting changes.

Can he change? It all depends on how you define change. Your family member or friend may have decided to remain with her abuser because his physical abuse has stopped. (This is not unheard of; although many abusive relationships become more violent over time, some do not. Some abusers *do* stop beating their victims, because they have discovered that they can get into big trouble with the law.) Your friend or relative may be hoping that this change is a step in the right direction; since he has proven he can control the punches and rapes, in the future he will learn how to control the insults and threats. But if the abuser still has the underlying need to control his victim, still feels that he is entitled to do so, this will not happen. Most abused women report that even when the *physical* abuse stops, the *psychologi-*

cal abuse does not. As a result, they never feel that they can let their guard down. They never feel safe in their own homes.

You can be helpful by understanding that abusers do not abuse because someone "pushed their buttons." You can understand that abusers always minimize or justify their abuse. You can realize that an abuser will not change unless he wants to change, and that this is highly unlikely.

It is frustrating to watch someone mistreat a person you care about. You might agree with the crusty old grandfather of one woman, who described his granddaughter's abusive husband as "lower than whale shit on the bottom of the ocean." You might be sorely tempted to teach him some manners, accompanied by your 350-pound baby brother, an offensive lineman for the Green Bay Packers. But not only does this sort of response not work, it also puts people at risk. Your role is not to change him (you can't) or to threaten him (you shouldn't) but to help her. The rest of this book will explain how.

CHECKLIST 3: WHAT WOULD IT TAKE FOR AN ABUSER TO CHANGE?

HE WOULD HAVE TO...	FOR EXAMPLE...
Admit fully to his history of psychological, sexual, and physical abusiveness toward any current or past partners he has abused. Acknowledge that the abuse was wrong, unconditionally.	He identifies the justifications he tends to use. He talks in detail about why his behaviors were unacceptable without slipping back into defending them.
Acknowledge that his behavior was a choice, not a loss of control.	He recognizes that there is a moment during each incident when he gives himself permission to become abusive.
Recognize the effects his abuse has had on his victim and her children, and show empathy.	He talks in detail about the short- and long-term impact that his abuse has had (fear, loss of trust, anger) but does not complain about the impact on *him*.
Identify in detail his pattern of controlling behaviors and entitled attitudes.	He precisely describes all the tactics he used to control her. He talks about the underlying beliefs and values that made him think he was entitled to control her.
Develop respectful behaviors and attitudes to replace the abusive ones he is stopping.	He listens carefully during conflicts. He demonstrates that she has rights and that they are equal to his.
Reevaluate his distorted image of her, replacing it with a more positive and empathic view.	He recognizes that he has mental habits of focusing on her weaknesses as a way to justify abusing her. He pays attention to her strengths and abilities.
Make amends for the damage he has done.	He is consistently kind and supportive, putting his own needs on the back burner. He pays for objects he has destroyed. He apologizes to others he has misled about his abusive acts.
Accept the consequences of his actions.	He stops blaming her for problems that are the result of his abuse, such as her loss of sexual desire or the fact that he is on probation.
Commit to not repeating his abusive behaviors and honor that commitment.	He places no conditions on his improvement (e.g., "I won't call you names as long as you don't raise your voice to me."). If he backslides, he does not justify his new abuse (e.g., "But I've done great for five months; what do you want from me?").
Accept the need to give up his privileges and do so.	He stops taking off for the weekend with his buddies while she is forced to stay home with the children. He no longer has affairs.
Accept that overcoming abusiveness is likely to be a life-long process.	He does not complain that he is sick of hearing about his abuse and that "It's time to get past all that." He recognizes that she may feel the effects of his past behavior for years.
Is willing to be accountable for his actions, both past and future.	He no longer believes that he is beyond reproach; instead, he accepts feedback about his behavior. If he backslides, he is willing to examine his actions and make changes.

Talking and Listening

Can We Talk?

Now that you understand physical abuse, psychological abuse, and abusers, what should you do next? Flushed and triumphant with your newly acquired knowledge, you feel ready to take immediate action. You itch to pick up the phone, call your friend or relative, and say, "Guess what? I have it all figured out. You know that skunk you're living with? He's an abuser! Your problem is more than a lousy relationship; it's domestic abuse! I'll be over in a few minutes to help you pack. We're getting you out of there. Today!"

Don't. This is a discussion that takes planning.

As you plan, remember that an abuser always controls and devalues his partner's perception of reality by making her doubt what she sees and hears. This has probably been going on for years. She needs support and encouragement to hold firmly to her own truth.

Helping her hold on to her truth may sound like a worthy goal, but how do you accomplish such a thing? You do it by talking about *your* perceptions and listening to *hers*. You may have some perspective on her relationship that she does not; your outside view allows you to see the big picture. But she knows things about her relationship that you do not; her inside view allows her to see details that you know nothing about. Whether or not she is insightful about the full extent of her predicament, she surely knows that she is in a tough situation. For example, one woman told me that her husband's physical attacks were always sneaky, without warning, so she was unable to duck, brace herself, or hide. She did not see herself as a victim of domestic abuse until years after she left, but she knew that he terrified her and she knew that she had to get away. She confided in her brother. Fortunately, he listened.

The person you care about may have already confided in you. You may have had endless conversations that left you feeling drained, steamed, or ready to tear your hair out. It might be, though, that you have not talked. Perhaps you tried once, and your efforts were gently (or not so gently) rejected. Or perhaps she tentatively dropped a hint, and you, feeling out of your depth, immediately changed the subject. Perhaps you and she have wordlessly agreed to treat her relationship like the proverbial elephant in the middle of the living room; if we all ignore the beast, it will simply wander away.

Avoiding the Pitfalls

It is difficult to talk about domestic abuse. How do you discuss such a sensitive subject without making your friend or relative feel worse than she already does and without causing her defenses to snap down, tight as hurricane shutters? As you consider the best way to approach your family member, friend, neighbor, or coworker, be careful to avoid two common pitfalls, *naming* and *blaming*.

Pitfall #1: Naming

If you begin by saying "You're a battered woman!" your discussion will be over before it starts. She will reply "I am not!" and that will be that. This *does not* mean that your family member or friend is in denial, a phrase I have come to loathe for its complacent emptiness. She may, however, refuse to accept that she is being battered.

"I'll believe it when I see it," the old expression goes, yet with domestic abuse the opposite is true. We *see* it when we *believe* it. Seeing is not the eye receiving pictures of what is in front of it but rather the brain reaching out to grasp the essence of those pictures. It is dreadful for her to imagine that the man she lives with could possibly be choosing his words and actions with particular care toward a deliberate end, to control her. Who could believe such a thing?

Consider it from her point of view. She has been dealing with an ongoing, relentless campaign of physical and psychological tactics for a long, long time. But that's not all she's been doing. She has also been living her life: working, raising children, meeting social obligations. She has been managing, more or less, to keep her head above water. Now you come along, and you have the nerve to sit there and call her a *battered woman*?

Besides, she truly doesn't think of herself as one of "those" women. A battered woman ends up on a hospital gurney with a knife in her ribs. A battered woman is a loser. She thinks of herself as a woman who has it all together. Sure, she has problems at home. Who doesn't? Yes, her husband or boyfriend is difficult—okay, nasty—terrifying, if you want to know the truth. But he isn't an abuser.

We see it when we believe it. When the time comes that she *does* believe it, she will see it all by herself. "It was as though a fog lifted," one woman told me. "I looked at him, and suddenly it was like I was seeing him for the first time," said another. Until that time comes, if you want to help her, don't let your conversation crumble into an argument about whether or not her relationship is abusive. It is perfectly possible to discuss domestic abuse without naming it.

Pitfall #2: Blaming

In her marvelous novel *The Sparrow,* Mary Doria Russell sums up the primary reason why we blame victims for the actions of those who victimize them. Put simply, we do so because we want to feel safe; we cannot bear the thought that if they are like us, then we might become victims, too. The book's main character explains, "He wanted it to be my fault, somehow.... It's human nature. He wanted it to be some mistake I made that he wouldn't have made, some flaw in me he didn't share, so he could believe it wouldn't have happened to him. But it wasn't my fault."

By this time, you know enough about domestic abuse that you would never blame your family member or friend for her partner's actions. You know that no matter what she did, she does not deserve to be abused. But victims of domestic abuse can be blamed in another way. They are often blamed for tolerating their situation. "Why do you put up with it?" her friends and relatives ask. "If my husband ever pulled the kind of garbage your husband does, I'd break both his legs...and he knows it!"

To an abused woman, these messages of blame are entirely consistent with similar messages she is already getting at home. Heaps of them. Many come from her abuser. If only she weren't such a slut, if only she weren't so dumb, if only she could please him in bed, if only she could cook a decent meal, then he wouldn't blow up at her. Some blame may come from her children. Abusers are expert manipulators, able with a few carefully chosen words, to thoroughly confuse their children about who is responsible for the tension in the home. "Mommy doesn't act right," he may say. "She ought to see a shrink. You should tell her to be nice to me." And the children often do. "Why do you have to make Daddy so mad?" they will ask. "Why can't you just do what he wants, and then he'll be happy?" Finally, ironically, no one blames an abused woman more severely than she blames herself. After hearing from her abuser repeatedly how worthless she is, she begins to believe it. Why would he say such things to her if they weren't true? If she could just get it right, she thinks, then he would treat her well.

Until you began educating yourself about domestic abuse, you might have thought that, in her shoes, you would have left after the first insult, the first threat, or, at the very least, the first slap. You might have found it difficult to keep from passing judgment on her, just as she passes judgment on herself. But domestic abuse is complicated, and leaving an abuser is never a simple act. Trust me. An abused woman spends an awful lot of time weighing her options. Just because she has not yet ended the relationship does not mean that she is a wimp, a dope, or a masochist. If you want to help your family member or friend, be sure there is no blame in your words, your look, your tone of voice, or your heart.

Starting the Conversation

Whether this is your first discussion with your family member or friend, or one of many, your approach will set the tone for the rest of the conversation. As you plan your approach, consider the time and place. If you and she are on a crowded bus, at the family's annual Fourth of July barbecue, or smack in the middle of her crowded kitchen with a tangle of crying toddlers underfoot, it is unlikely that she will be particularly forthcoming.

Plan how you will open the discussion. This may seem a little forced for your taste, but it is important. Unless you are a mental health professional, there is no reason why you would know how to have this sort of conversation. Prepare a little script for yourself. Rehearse in front of the mirror until it feels natural. The script can be pretty short; the simplest words often have the greatest power. You can never go wrong by starting with the words "I'm worried about you."

Here's why. In Chapter 2, you learned that abusers use a variety of tactics to control their partners. One tactic used almost universally is *isolation*. It works because a woman who has been isolated from family members and friends is unlikely to go to them for support. If you start the conversation with the words "I'm worried about you," you may be the first person in a long time to express concern.

For example, consider this conversation between Lynn, a fifth-grade teacher, and Dee, a third-grade teacher in the same school. Lynn and her boyfriend sometimes meet Dee and her husband Keith for a movie and a beer. Last night, Lynn saw something that made her realize she had to start a conversation with her coworker:

Lynn: Dee, *I'm worried about you.*

Dee: Huh? What are you talking about?

Lynn: Last night, when the four of us were driving to the movie, I happened to look in my rearview mirror at the traffic behind me. I didn't mean to see it, but Keith raised the back of his hand to you and had a really mean scowl on his face. You immediately stopped talking. And you got a real "Uh-oh" look on your face, like you were afraid of him. *That made me worried about you.*

Dee: (Laughing) That? Oh, heavens, that was nothing! Keith was just kidding around! You completely misinterpreted it!

Lynn: Well, good. I'm glad. And I wouldn't have said anything, except it isn't the first time I've seen Keith do something that made me nervous. Last month, when you were talking to Jack at the Christmas party, Keith grabbed your arm really hard and marched you to the other side of the room. A few of us noticed it. And it makes me feel uncomfortable the way

Keith calls you "Dee-Dee dumb-dumb." I know he smiles, like it's a joke and you laugh it off, but it's insulting. I mean, the last thing you are is dumb! You're the best teacher in the whole school! I'm your friend, hon, and I'll drop it if you want me to, but I care about you and I just had to tell you that *I'm worried about you.*

There are a few points to notice in the above conversation. First, Lynn repeated the phrase "I'm worried about you" three times. That repetition was deliberate; when someone becomes defensive, as your friend or relative is likely to do, she probably will not hear you unless you repeat your words several times. The only message Lynn really wants Dee to take away is the fact that Lynn is worried. Second, Lynn was careful to spell out Keith's behavior concretely. He raised his hand to Dee. He scowled. He grabbed her arm. He called her "Dee-Dee dumb-dumb." Specifics are always better than global statements like "Keith is a jerk" or "He's a mean guy." Third, although Dee minimized Keith 's behavior, which victims generally do, Lynn did not attempt to argue. Instead, she simply gave a few more examples of Keith 's upsetting acts, reinforced her concern, stated one final time that she was worried, and sat back to listen to whatever Dee might want to tell her.

So now Lynn has started the conversation. It can't have been easy for her, since she and Dee work together. But the real question is, what's going to happen next? There are several possibilities. The first is that Dee will pack her bags and leave Keith this afternoon. Problem solved. I hold out no hope whatsoever that Dee will do anything of the sort. In fact, it would probably be a *very* bad idea! Every woman who is leaving an abuser needs to do some serious planning. She may need to put measures in place to ensure her safety and the safety of her children. (More about this in Chapter 6.) Certainly, she will want to arrange her finances, her housing, her health insurance, and all the other details of her life. If you have ever moved to another city or even around the corner, you know what a tedious, aggravating, tense, and time-consuming job it is. Now imagine doing all that work while looking over your shoulder. For an abused woman, leaving her abuser in a planned and orderly way is not just a good idea—it may save her life.

Or something entirely different may happen when Lynn tells Dee that she's worried about her. Dee will tell Lynn about a few more incidents—the late-night arguments that she could swear Keith deliberately initiates on the night before the school principal is coming into her classroom to watch her teach—the times she has caught him reading her e-mail messages—the night he threatened her with a loaded gun.

There is a third option, the one most likely to happen to Lynn, and to you. Dee will politely thank Lynn for her interest and make it clear that everything at home is just peachy. Then she will swallow her last sip of coffee, go into her classroom, and take attendance. And that will be that...except it won't. Dee will think about Lynn's words. Not right away perhaps, and not all the time, but she *will* think about them. She will repeat them, her own private mantra. "My friend from work is worried about me," she may muse. And slowly, gradually, she might begin to feel worried about herself. At some future date, she may come back to Lynn, ready to talk about her marriage. Or she may not. Perhaps she knows someone else with whom she can talk more easily than she can to Lynn. She may feel uncomfortable discussing intimate family matters with someone she sees every day at work. Instead, she may have a few talks with a dear friend who is a social worker. She may confide in her uncle when she is in his city on a business trip.

Does this mean that Lynn must now sit quietly by, never raising the subject of Keith's behavior again unless Dee brings it up? Since they are coworkers, that's probably exactly what Lynn ought to do unless she sees or hears something else that makes her believe Dee is in danger. (Of course, if Lynn were Dee's mother, she couldn't possibly drop the matter; she would keep trying to talk to her daughter. Even then, she would have to be careful not to drive Dee away.) No matter what comes of this initial conversation, though, Lynn's decision to speak up made a difference. She introduced the possibility of change into Dee's life simply by saying, "I'm worried about you."

Like Dee, your friend or relative probably will not respond immediately to voiced concerns. Accept that you may never know the impact of your words. Say the words anyway. Several years ago, I had a friend whose marriage did not seem right to me. In fact, I thought the guy was trouble the minute I met him, long before they were engaged. But she was in love, so what can you do? I saw her pretty frequently during the five years of her marriage. I was already working in this field, and whenever she would tell me something that he did (which did not appear to be physical abuse, but sure seemed to be making her unhappy), I would say things to her like "Are you okay?" and "That really doesn't seem right to me" and "It was nasty of him to say that" and "If it feels wrong, then you're right." Because she had married at the age of 35, because she was deeply committed to making her marriage work, my friend spent a great deal of energy justifying and explaining her husband's actions. So my goal was simple: to *not normalize* his behavior. She finally had enough and kicked him out. I will never forget her words. "You know, Elaine, I knew what you were telling me. You thought I didn't hear you, and you thought I was ignoring you. Believe me, I wasn't. I wasn't able to act on it yet, but if you had said nothing, I would have *really* thought I was crazy. Because you said something, I knew I wasn't."

Words That Help

Your discussions with your family member or friend will probably go well beyond "I'm worried about you." You may be the first person in a long time that she has felt she can talk to. Her stories may bubble up, or she may have trouble finding the right words. A tango begins with a single step, then gradually progresses to interlocking and increasingly intricate patterns. Like a tango, your conversations will be everchanging dances. Your first talk will lead to others, especially after she realizes that you understand some of what she is going through, that you do not blame her for tolerating his behavior, and that you will not pressure her to leave.

What you talk about is really up to her. She may want to describe past abusive episodes in her relationship so that you can more fully appreciate her current dilemma. She may appreciate your analysis of her partner's actions as she struggles to sort out what's really going on in her life. She may want to bounce ideas off you as she plans for her future. But, no matter what specific aspects of her situation you and she discuss, certain words can always help.

"What is this like for you?"

It has become a cliché that listening is more important than speaking, that we have two ears and one mouth for a reason. If you want to help a victim of domestic abuse, though, it's true. You can never go wrong by asking her, "What is this like for *you*?" and then listening carefully to what she tells you. There may come a time when she asks for your advice; there may come a time when it's appropriate for you to give it. But unless you have legal, medical, or social services training, or unless you have successfully escaped from an abuser, don't be too quick to tell her what to do. Your advice is probably no better than that of any other well-meaning person.

I know that sounds pretty harsh. But think about it. Unless you have experienced domestic abuse, you can imagine but your heart can't truly encompass the emotional tangle that comes from living with the misrepresentations, mixed messages, and impossible demands of an abuser. You can imagine but your muscles can't really feel the stress of tiptoeing through the minefield of each day, never knowing which words, actions, or even facial expressions will trigger an explosion.

Karen Wilson, domestic violence activist and author of the book *When Violence Begins at Home*, writes that to help a victim of domestic abuse we must *listen with love*. Listening with love is a gift, Karen believes, because it goes against our natural tendency to establish our own position. If you jump in to make suggestions without taking the time to listen with love, then you are—ironically—acting remarkably like the man who is abusing your friend or relative. He already makes all her decisions for her. He tells her that she is incapable of showing good judgment, that she has made a mess of her life, and that if he weren't there to tell her what to do she'd fall flat on her face.

Your intentions are not the same as his, of course. Your suggestions are for her own good. But she has likely been under his thumb for so long that, in her mind, there may appear to be very little difference. ("But I *do* listen!" I can hear you wailing. I'm sure you do. But think of the times you sprinkle your discussions with phrases like "If I were you," "You should just," and, the real kicker, "I just can't understand why you won't...")

You can never go wrong if you ask her, "What is this like for *you?*" Every abused woman experiences abuse differently. One woman's husband might fly into a jealous rage whenever she is 10 minutes late. Another might not care what time she comes home, but heaven help her if she voices her own opinion on how their money should be spent. So it is important to listen for *her* sake, both to show that you respect her and to create a safe place for her to shape her thoughts and feelings. Listening is also important for *your* sake. You may have seen or heard a few things that made you concerned for her safety; that's why you started the conversation. To be helpful, though, you need more information.

Some people believe that abused women are bald-faced liars, that they blithely pretend there is no abuse in their lives, and that if they are asked about it directly, they look you straight in the eye and deny everything. In many cases, though, an abused woman is quite willing to discuss her situation *if* she believes the person who asked the question is prepared to deal with her answer. Listening with love is one way to assure your friend or relative that you can handle whatever she cares to tell you. Even if it turns out that listening is all you *can* do, you have done a great deal.

"You don't deserve this."

I have had the privilege—I use the term loosely—of observing some batterer treatment groups in session. I could never lead such groups. I have enormous respect for the people who do.

Picture a room that looks vaguely institutional, a high school class-room, perhaps, or the room where you took your driver's license exam. Metal chairs are arranged in a wobbly circle. About 15 men have draped themselves in various positions across these chairs, the expressions on their faces ranging from discomfort to boredom to wry amusement. They are the "clients," convicted batterers. A woman and a man—trained facilitators—have posted tonight's discussion question on a flip chart: "What Causes Abuse?" They are looking for answers like entitlement, control, and power. These are important concepts they have spent countless sessions teaching, discussing, and role-playing. The perpetrators are having none of it. They want to talk about how their wives and girlfriends victimize *them*.

For one screwy minute, I forget everything I know about domestic abuse and actually feel a twinge of sympathy for these guys. This one's girlfriend was drunk, she threw a teakettle at him, he ducked, the teakettle bounced off the wall back at her face, the cops came, and he got arrested. That one's wife didn't clean the house, so then he yelled, so then she smacked him, so then he smacked her back, so then the cops came, and he got arrested. Story follows story, each man eager to explain what *she* did, oddly silent about what *he* did.

Eventually, one of the facilitators calls a halt to the righteous recital. "What's going on here?" she asks. The men exchange sidelong glances, grinning sheepishly. "Playing the bitch tape!" they singsong. I give myself a little shake; the room comes back into focus, and I remember that abusers always deny responsibility for their actions. I can't help wondering, though; how long will these guys remember the lesson? What will happen the next time one of them decides that his wife or girlfriend is being a bitch? Will he push the "off" button on the tape player, as the facilitators have taught? Or will he allow the tape to keep rolling, minute after long minute, until he convinces himself—and her—that she deserves everything she's about to get?

This is why it can be so helpful to tell your family member or friend in no uncertain terms that no matter what she might have done to *him*, she does not deserve what he is doing to *her*. She may have said or done any number of things that make her feel ashamed of herself. These might be trivial, such as allowing the children to make too much noise when daddy wants to watch his favorite reality television show. They might be less trivial. Perhaps she promised to bring the car to the repair shop and failed to keep her promise. Any of us would feel let down if someone disappointed us like that; most of us would not respond by locking our partner in the bathroom for three days.

It is terribly difficult for a woman in an abusive relationship to see the mismatch between her mistakes—even assuming they *are* mistakes—and her abuser's response to them. A friend of mine told her sister, "You haven't done anything that any of the rest of us haven't done a million times. But the rest of us don't get beaten up over it." This is the message an abused woman needs to hear, not that she is perfect—no one is—but that no matter *what* she has done, she does not deserve to be abused.

"You're in a tough situation."

Well, *of course* she's in a tough situation, you might be thinking. She doesn't need me to point out the obvious, does she? Actually, she might. Framing her situation as complex accomplishes two things: it lets *her* know it, and it lets her know that *you* know it.

When you're up to your fanny in alligators, as the old expression goes, it's hard to remember that your original objective was to drain the swamp. A woman in an abusive relationship is often so busy trying to keep herself safe while juggling the other parts of her life that she cannot step back and clearly see the entire picture.

She may, for example, feel stuck in her relationship because she cannot see how she and the children can manage without her partner's income. (This is not only a problem for women who do not work outside the home; many abused women who are employed still have no access to family finances.) Your family member or friend may feel so trapped financially that she has lost sight of the fact that she has good job skills. To some extent, her abuser has set this up. "You'll never make it without me," he may have told her, until she has come to believe it. His litany drones endlessly in her ears, even when he is not around. "You're a worthless, stupid, clumsy excuse for a woman. You can't even string 10 words together to make a sentence. If your I.Q. were any lower, we'd have to water you twice a week. The best job you could ever get would be flipping burgers at MacDonald's." Never mind that she has a responsible position in the marketing department of a medical supply company; if someone tells you often enough that you are an incompetent fool, you will begin to feel like one.

Some abused women—particularly the ones who already recognize that their relationships are abusive and are attempting to find a way to break free—already know *exactly* how tough their situation is. They have already thought long and hard about the barriers that stand in their way. They may have explored a variety of options for overcoming some of these barriers. They may have discovered that some barriers are taller and thicker than the Great Wall of China.

A woman once wrote to me, desperately seeking help for her sister who lives in Canada. The sister is married to a man from another country. They have a daughter who, born in Canada, is a Canadian citizen. It's complicated; the mother *is* a Canadian citizen, the father is *not* a citizen, or maybe it's the other way around. At any rate, the woman who wrote to me, who is a United States citizen, wants to help her sister escape from Canada with the baby to get away from her husband, who has promised to kill her if she leaves. Canadian customs says no dice; the child cannot leave the country without the father's permission, even though the father poses a serious threat to the child's mother. This sounds like a movie script, doesn't it? Except it isn't. This is really happening in the beginning of the 21st century in North America.

I hope your family member or friend is not facing a situation this complex and terrifying, but many women who are attempting to get away from an abuser must deal with problems that seem hopeless. Sometimes the best way to be helpful is to untangle the individual threads of her fears.

You could, for example, tenderly say something like this: "I can see you're in a tough situation. It's not easy to figure out the best thing to do. You're worried about moving out because you don't want your kids to have to go to a different school. You're also worried about whether you can find an apartment you can afford. So the thought of leaving is scary. But staying is scary, too. You're worried that the way he treats you is starting to affect the kids' behavior at school. And you're afraid that the next time he hits you, he might really hurt you. It's a real dilemma; I can understand why it's so hard to decide whether to stay or leave."

"You're a strong person."

You can never go wrong telling an abused woman that she is a strong person. She may not feel particularly strong. She may feel ashamed, guilty, stupid, or a complete failure. But when you tell her she is strong, you are telling her the truth.

Remember the stereotype of an abused woman—a weak little mouse, cowering in the corner, waiting helplessly for her next beating. If this image bears no resemblance to your friend or relative, don't be surprised; most abused women are not passive victims. They show enormous strength, both while they are within the relationship and as they work to extricate themselves. One proof of this strength is the huge number of women who do, ultimately, manage to break free and go on with their lives. These women do not wait, like Rapunzel in her tower, to be rescued. They rescue themselves. They are resourceful. They fight back. They take care of themselves and, often, of their children.

I met many strong women when I did the research for an earlier book, *Surviving Domestic Violence: Voices of Women Who Broke Free.* One woman saved dimes from her grocery money to accumulate enough bus fare so she and her son could escape from her violent husband who would, she was certain, murder her if he knew of her plans. (I use the word "escape" deliberately. No woman ever "leaves" an abuser. Leaving is what you do when the movie is over.) Every abused woman, whether she has escaped from her abuser or not, is strong. She has to be strong to survive her abuser's ongoing campaign of control, to survive his daily assaults on her spirit and dignity.

But What if She...

Conversations about domestic abuse are not easy conversations to have. Most of the time, you can count on your innate common sense and your new understanding of domestic abuse. However, two special situations may come up at some point.

- She may defend him. This sounds terrible, doesn't it? All your good words have come to naught! She's sliding backwards! You want to grab her by the shoulders and remind her what a jackass he is! But that's exactly the wrong thing to do.

- She may trash him. That sounds great, doesn't it? All your good words have paid off! She's finally seeing him for the jackass he is! You want to grab her in a big bear hug and cheer her on! But that's exactly the wrong thing to do.

What if She Defends Him?

She starts to waffle. It may be during your first conversation, your fifth, or your umpteenth. She's been thinking it over; maybe she's given you the wrong impression of her relationship. She's no angel, you know. And that time he lost his temper and she got those bruises, it really wasn't his fault. His boss had been giving him a bad time that week. He called a sitter for the kids the very next night, he took her out to dinner, and they had a long heart-to-heart talk. He promised to do a better job of managing his anger. She can see he's really trying to do it, too. He's been sweet to her for an entire month.

Now is when you have to take a deep breath, let it out slowly, and swallow all those words that are perched on the tip of your tongue— (Dummy! Dope! Have you totally lost what's left of your tiny mind? Don't you remember all the things this man has done to you over the past seven years? Ork! If you can understand why she defends him, you will be able to muster up a more useful response.

The very nature of an abusive relationship sets the victim up to believe that her abuser is actually her best friend and that people such as you, who are trying to help her, are actually her enemies. You may have heard the term Stockholm Syndrome to describe this phenomenon, which was first identified during a 1973 bank holdup in Stockholm, Sweden. Two bank robbers held a man and three women hostage for six days. During those six days, the victims came to believe that their captors were really their saviors and that the police were their enemies.

To see how the Stockholm Syndrome works in abusive relationships, let's compare a victim of domestic violence with a woman on a hijacked airplane. There are three important similarities.

1. **Both women are isolated.** The hijacked woman has no connection with the outside world. Her only information comes from the hijackers. She has no idea whether she will be rescued, whether her government will negotiate with the hijackers, or whether anyone on the outside even knows what is happening to her. The abused woman may not look isolated—she goes to work, she visits the library, and she takes the kids to band practice—but in all the important ways, her abuser has isolated her from friends, family, and anyone else who might otherwise speak up, including you.

2. **Both women feel trapped.** The hijacked woman is trapped. She may, of course, make an attempt to escape. But if she does, she may die...and she knows it. An abused woman feels trapped. She is probably not locked in the attic, but her abuser may have made her feel as threatened as the woman on the plane, saying something like "If I can't have you, then no one can" or "Leave if you want to, but you'll never see the kids again."

3. **Both women experience occasional acts of kindness.** The hijackers will sometimes treat the woman on the plane nicely, allowing her to use the bathroom and permitting flight attendants to distribute food. This is also a common abuser tactic. Most abused women report that their partners are capable of occasional sweet gestures that raise their hopes again and again...until the next time.

These three factors—isolation, feeling trapped, and occasional acts of kindness—can leave her feeling guilty for talking to you, which she sees as a betrayal. When she starts to feel guilty, she defends him. What she is actually doing is telling you to back off. And so you must, with a smile and a friendly pat on her shoulder. But don't take it personally, and leave the door open.

You could, for example, say something like this: "I'm so glad that things are more peaceful at home. I've been worried about you." Then drop the whole business. But continue to remain in contact with her so she knows you are available when she is ready. Chances are good that at some point she will want to talk again.

What if She Trashes Him?

The second tricky situation is the flip side of the first. She doesn't defend him—she trashes him. And you're ecstatic. Hooray! She finally sees him for the slime he is. She comes over to your house, furious with him. Boy, do you want to agree with her! Boy, do you want to say something like, "I'm so glad you've finally seen it! I never liked the guy. I never understood what you saw in him. He's a total loser. Thank heavens you've finally come to your senses! Now you can get on with your life."

Uh-uh. Because next week, or next month, he will talk her back into the relationship with glowing promises or veiled threats. He may apologize profusely for his actions. He may promise to start therapy and may actually do it. He may threaten to come after her if she doesn't move back home. Whatever tactics he uses, chances are good that she will return to him. And then she'll remember all the bad things you said about him. (I know, I know. She said them too. She's feeling guilty about being disloyal, so she doesn't want to remember that part.)

And the door slams shut. She will be reluctant to confide in you again because now she sees you as the enemy, the person who criticized her man. Remember, breaking free of abuse is a process. You want to be available to her *throughout* that process. Even though it's tough, don't agree with her when she's trashing him. Instead of focusing on *him*, focus on *her*. The conversation could go something like this.

Her: I've had it with Michael! Last night he pushed me out the bedroom door in the middle of the night and locked it just because I wouldn't have the kind of sex he likes. I had to sleep on the couch and make up some excuse to tell the kids in the morning. I doubt they believed me.

You: That must have been terribly embarrassing.

Her: It sure was! I hate it when he gets so crazy.

You: It sounds like it's hard for you when things like that happen.

Her: It's really hard. I wish I could just move out, but I don't have any money saved to rent an apartment. We have a joint checking account, but he never tells me how much is in it.

You: Wow, what a tough position to be in, wanting to leave but being so short of funds.

Notice, you say nothing about what an insensitive boor Michael was for locking her out of the bedroom. In fact, you never mention Michael at all! You simply listen carefully and restate what she is telling you. This may not sound like a big deal. You would much prefer to write a check for her first month's rent. And you would dearly love to march over to Michael's office, wielding your heaviest frying pan, and teach the man some manners. But the fact is that you can provide a valuable service. And you can do it without saying anything negative about Michael.

She will probably not leave Michael immediately. Leaving is always a process. But because you have shown her that you care about *her* while remaining carefully neutral about *Michael*, you have kept the door open for future conversations.

The Power of Words
Words are not always enough. In order to escape safely, your family member or friend may have to meet with domestic violence advocates or counselors, police detectives, doctors, lawyers, or social workers. She may need to find emergency housing. She may require the services of a domestic violence advocate. She may even need to seek temporary refuge and support in a battered woman's shelter. The next

chapter will explain what you can do to connect her with these resources.

But your actions can't come out of the blue. Unless you believe that she is in immediate danger (more about this in Chapter 6), you can't simply swoop down and take charge of her life. A woman sent me a compelling letter, reflecting on the role her family and friends played as she struggled to escape from her abusive husband. She wrote, "I found that the more people pushed, even though they meant well, the more hesitant I was. Family and friends need to love us for who we are now. Not who they want us to be, or who we once were. Because if they do that, we become stronger by realizing that we are already lovable and don't have to change to be loved."

When a victim of domestic abuse visualizes breaking free of her abuser, she asks herself two questions. First she wonders, will I be better off if I leave? Once she determines that she will be better off, her second question is, can I do it? She must answer these questions for herself, but your words have the power to support her through the process. Your words can help her to name her situation as abusive. They can help her articulate the physical and emotional damage she has endured at the hands of her abuser. They can help her develop insight about her options. They can help her weigh her alternatives and decide what to do. Finally, most importantly, your words can bear witness to her struggles and her strength.

After my lecture to a class of first-year medical students, one woman wanted to talk with me. The two of us sat outside on a bench; she talked, I listened. "I feel like I'm going through life balanced on my big toe," she said. She and her husband only saw each other on occasional weekends. He was commuting between Salt Lake City, where she attended medical school, and Los Angeles, where he was completing a Ph.D. program at UCLA. Each time he left Utah for California, she could breathe freely again. When he came home for a visit, she felt the walls closing in on her, until she found herself doing a countdown to the hour when she'd drive him to the airport. Her husband was fond of sitting her down and explaining why he believed that she was mentally ill. He would enumerate each piece of evidence: her tears (hysteria!), her concerns about money (paranoid delusions), and her diminished interest in sex (frigidity). She knew it was pure nonsense. Of course she did, except for the part of her that worried he might be right.

After listening carefully, this is what I said to her. "You seem eminently sane to me. You seem to be seeing things extremely clearly. You seem tired—you seem sad—but you don't seem the least bit crazy." She took in a deep breath, letting it out again in a single puff. Then she turned to me and said, "You just helped me more than you will ever know."

Taking Action

Going Beyond Conversation

In the previous chapter, you learned how to talk and how to listen. These are crucial ways to help an abused woman. But they may not be enough. You may also need to take action.

It's all very well to say that a victim of domestic abuse needs to sort through her options on her own. In most cases, I agree with this viewpoint. But let's not take all this autonomy too far. My mother and I recently discussed philosophies of child rearing. When I was born, parents were taught to be fully involved in their kids' lives from birth through the late teen years, then to back firmly off once these selfsame kids became adults. An interfering parent was the worst possible insult to someone of Mom's generation. "I wonder if we were right, though," my mother mused. "After all, if you saw your daughter in a burning building and you could tell that she didn't realize her own danger, you'd certainly rush in and yank her out. Why should it be any different if you see her in an abusive marriage and you can tell that she doesn't understand how bad it is?" Yes, exactly.

Sometimes, the building is on fire and you need to take action. This chapter will discuss three ways you can take action to help your family member or friend: assessing her danger, planning for her safety, and sorting through the community resources that are set up to support abused women.

Assessing Her Danger

Donna, Claire, and Wendy knew that the person lying in the hospital bed was Liz, but they could not recognize her. Her eyes swollen shut, her head swollen to twice its normal size, she looked precisely like the victim of an auto accident—until they saw the purple strangulation necklace around her neck, Jay's parting gift before he calmly removed the receivers from the telephones, hid her purse, and left her on the kitchen floor to die. "Call an ambulance," she begged. "Don't do this to your children!" He looked down at her dispassionately. "Nah, the kids will be fine. They'll be better off without you." Had Liz not remembered that her cell phone was in her car, had she not managed to crawl to the garage and dial 9-1-1 before she passed out, her three best friends would have been attending her funeral that afternoon rather than sitting in her hospital room, trying to come to terms with what had happened to their best friend, trying to decide what they ought to do.

CHECKLIST 4: HOW DANGEROUS IS THIS ABUSER?

RISK FACTOR	RED FLAGS
Past Violence	He seriously injured the victim in the past. He injured other people in the past. He physically abused the victim when she was pregnant. He sexually assaulted the victim.
Current Violence	His violence has recently escalated. He is stalking, monitoring, or harassing the victim. He is violent outside of the home, either to her or to others. He is violent toward family pets.
Children	He is violent toward children. He is sexually abusive toward children. He is not the father of her children. He believes that he is not the father of her children.
Threats	He threatened to kill the victim. He threatened to kill himself. He threatened the victim's friends or family members. He has access to weapons, especially firearms. He recently acquired a firearm.
Substance Abuse	He uses drugs, especially PCP, crack, cocaine, or speed. He drinks heavily.
Leaving	He suspects the victim is planning to leave. The victim has already left.

You may never face a crisis of these proportions. I hope you do not. But should it happen, you will need to take immediate action. Throughout this book I recommend moving slowly with your family member or friend, taking the time to listen and talk, to establish a relationship of trust, before you and she work together to take action. Sometimes, this cautious, baby-step approach will not be possible.

Not all abused women are seriously injured or killed by their abusive partners, but some are. How can you tell if your family member or friend is at risk? It is impossible to predict for certain, of course, but most of the horror stories that blare on the evening news did not come out of the blue. There were warning signs. Checklist 4 is a summary of risk factors commonly associated with abuser violence. *If even a single one of these risk factors is present in her life, she may be in serious danger.*

Planning for Her Safety

Every abused woman, whether she is planning to leave her abuser or not, needs a safety plan for herself and her children. Every safety plan is different. For example, a woman who lives on the third floor of an apartment building with only a single entrance and no back door needs to consider how she will keep herself from being trapped inside the apartment. A woman with children needs to create a safety plan that includes a signal to her children to leave the house quickly and go someplace safe when their father's violence escalates.

You are probably *not* the person who should be helping her to create an individualized safety plan. Trained professionals can do a much better job. If she lives in a town or city with a domestic violence program or a battered women's shelter, this is the best place for her to get such help. If not, a variety of other agencies have counselors, social workers, and victim advocates on staff to create safety plans with their clients. In case you need to do some preliminary planning, though, and to give you a sense of what safety planning entails, Checklists 5, 6, and 7 show three sample safety plans.

Even if she never implements a safety plan, the act of creating the plan can help an abused woman feel that she is reclaiming her control. Simply getting a spare car key made and tucking it beneath a bush near the back door, hidden where only she can find it, can empower a woman who has had her power taken away. Equally empowering is her realization that when the violence starts, she is not completely helpless. For example, she can leave the bedroom, where his shotgun sits propped in the closet. She can keep away from the kitchen with its knives and heavy pots. She can avoid being trapped in the bathroom. Instead, if she sees the warning signs that his abuse is about to turn physical, she can innocuously shift herself to the living room, where the most dangerous object is the remote control.

CHECKLIST 5: PLANNING FOR SAFETY IF SHE STAYS WITH HER ABUSER

- Help her identify her support network and consider how she can use it in an emergency.

- Help her figure out a plan in advance for calling the police if the abuser becomes violent. If she can't get to a phone, can she work out a signal in advance with children, family, neighbors, or friends?

- Suggest that she think about the signs that let her know that his violence is about to escalate. What strategies have worked in the past to keep her safe or minimize injury?

- Help her plan how she and the children can escape from the house or apartment once she knows the violence is inevitable. Consider what precautions she can take to avoid being trapped.

- Help her establish a safe place where she and her children can hide for a few days.

- Suggest that she keep important items (purse, car keys, birth certificates, medication, immigration papers, childrens' fingerprints and photos, and credit cards) hidden where she can get to them quickly if she has to leave in a hurry.

- Be sure she keeps a cell phone with her at all times that is preprogrammed to dial the police.

- If there are firearms in the house or apartment, is there a way she can remove the ammunition without putting herself at risk?

- Encourage her to talk with her children about the violence at home, so they do not believe they are to blame.

CHECKLIST 6:
PLANNING FOR SAFETY IF HE IS REMOVED
FROM THE HOME OR SHE HAS LEFT

- Change locks on doors and windows.

- Install smoke detectors and ensure that fire extinguishers work.

- Purchase a rope ladder for escape from second-floor windows.

- Install a motion-sensitive outside lighting system.

- Keep a cell phone with you at all times that is preprogrammed to dial the police.

- Alert the school and all childcare providers that he is not permitted to see the children.

- Teach children how to use the telephone and make collect calls in case they are abducted.

- Take security measures at work, in public, and in the neighborhood. For example, give a copy of any protective order to a supervisor at work and a nearby neighbor, and ask them to call the police if they see him.

CHECKLIST 7: PLANNING FOR SAFETY DURING A VIOLENT INCIDENT

- Go to a low-risk space. Avoid being trapped in a room with no access to an outside door, such as a bathroom or a bedroom.

- Avoid a room with weapons, such as the bedroom, garage, basement, or kitchen.

- Make sure that your cell phone is in your pocket, preprogrammed to dial the police.

- Be alert to signs that an attack is coming. Try to avoid being drawn into physical combat.

- Get out of the house quickly through a door, window, elevator, rope ladder, or fire escape.

- Have a prearranged code word with the children to signal that they should escape from the house. Have escape drills in advance, so that they will know what to do.

- Arrange in advance with a nearby neighbor that the children can go there immediately.

Sorting Through the Resources

Perhaps there will come a time when a victim of domestic violence can march into one office, fill out a simple single-page form, and walk out with a divorce, full custody of her children, a financial settlement, a decent car, an affordable apartment, and her batterer safely behind bars. Until that time, a woman who finally summons up the courage to take a tentative first step toward freedom can be crushed when, trying to extricate herself from domestic abuse by herself, she bumps up against an obstacle.

This obstacle need not be especially large; in an abused woman's fragile state of mind, a pebble can loom large as a boulder. For example, I know a woman whose husband's irrational acts frightened her so badly that she decided she had better go to the police for advice. This was only her second visit to a police station; the first had been 13 years earlier on a field trip with her Brownie troop. During her earlier outing, Mr. Policeman had smiled encouragingly at the wide-eyed little girls. This time, Mr. Detective was curt and businesslike. She was devastated, nearly in tears at his lack of empathy. This woman eventually went to the domestic violence shelter in her town, received the appropriate information and support to free herself from her husband, returned to college, and has recently completed graduate work as a nurse practitioner. Time and professional training have taught her that the detective did everything he was supposed to do…and more. Police detectives don't have to empathize, though many do. Their job is to keep battered women from being killed. If you want empathy, you go to a social worker.

The bad news is that domestic abuse is complicated, your friend or relative's options are limited, and breaking free of domestic abuse is a lengthy process. The good news is that if you want to help her break free, you don't have to do it alone.

This was not always true. There was a time when, if an abused woman wanted to do something about her situation, she was on her own. The first shelters for battered women in the United States were established in the 1970s. (This is a fairly dismaying thought when you consider that the first animal shelter was established in Philadelphia more than a hundred years earlier, in 1869.) But times have changed. An abused woman, and someone like you who cares about her, can find plenty of help. There are many resources available at the local, state, and national levels.

Every resource can provide some part of what she needs. No single resource can do it all. This ought not to surprise us; after all, you wouldn't go to a shoe store and expect to buy a pair of red suede boots, a tube of mascara, an omelet pan, a monkey wrench and a bushel of oats. You would expect to drive around town for awhile. But an abused woman in search of community resources is under enormous pressure to get it all done quickly. This is where her local domestic violence program can help. The local program is set up to coordinate all the community resources so that victims need not do it on their own.

Robin Winner, Executive Director of Synergy Services, Inc., a large violence intervention agency providing services to victims, children, and perpetrators in Kansas City, stated in a letter to me, "Most well-run domestic violence programs can assist with most of a victim's needs: shelter, legal protection, attorney, case management, housing funds to get her started, household items, furniture, clothing, counseling for her and her children, peer support groups, spiritual support and healing. Some even offer job readiness training, childcare, yoga, massage, art and play therapy, and so on."

You can be helpful by finding out how to reach the domestic violence program in her area. The easiest way to do this is by calling the *National Domestic Violence Hotline* (800-799-SAFE). They are lovely people; I call them often. They do not ask for your name or hers. You simply tell them that you are worried about someone and that you are looking for local programs where she can go for help. They will ask what state and city she lives in. They may also ask other questions about her situation. Then they will give you program names, telephone numbers, and in some cases, the name of a contact person. If her state has its own domestic violence hotline, they will give you that number as well.

Ideally, *she* is the one who should be calling the National Domestic Violence Hotline. In fact, for many abused women, the process of making this call and following up in her community is empowering. I'm not alone! she says to herself. I've found people out there who want to help me! But if she is not ready to make this call, it does no harm for you to do the initial research.

Once you start digging, you will be surprised how much reference material is available, both at the state and local level. In some ways, it is safer for her if you are the one to collect this material. In her house, there is a risk that her abuser will discover it; as you now know, an abuser can become more violent if he suspects that his victim is planning to leave. Every state has a domestic violence hotline. Call the hotline in her state and ask them to send you whatever they have. While you're on the phone, ask them who you can call in her city or town that might also have pamphlets, brochures, or other reference materials.

You already realize that you can't tell her she has to leave, you can't do the leaving for her, and you can't make her abuser stop his behavior. But once she makes up her mind to take advantage of the domestic violence program in her area, you can take action. For example, her abuser may take her car, leaving her no way to keep appointments with a social worker or a lawyer. If you own a car and your schedule permits, you can drive her. In some communities, victims of domestic violence receive free public transportation. You can help her make these arrangements. She may be entitled to low-cost legal services. You can help her fill out the necessary forms.

Though the number of domestic violence programs is growing, it may be that your friend or relative lives in an area where no such program exists. In that case, look for a community-based support group for victims of domestic violence. The National Domestic Violence Hotline or her state hotline can provide this information. Another possibility is to contact a local mental health center; they should be able to refer her to people who can help her coordinate the resources she will need to escape.

You lead a rich and varied life. Although you care about your family member or friend and you want to help her, it cannot become your full-time job. By familiarizing yourself with the resources in her community that are set up to support victims of domestic violence, you will see that her problems need not take over your life. Your job is not to rescue her. In fact, you shouldn't. A rescuer believes that an abused woman is helpless and needs someone to save her. She does not need to be saved; she needs to be supported in her decisions. A supporter believes that an abused woman can use appropriate information and available resources to make her own decisions.

Law Enforcement Resources

The police are sometimes the first outsiders to have any contact with an abused woman. A neighbor hears an argument, a shot is fired, a child screams, and the next thing you know, two cops are at the door. Although police can and do save lives, it is important to have a realistic understanding of what they can offer to your friend or relative. I was invited to make a presentation at a medical school in Alabama. After my talk, a doctor approached me and said, "I have a patient whose husband beats her. I don't understand why she puts up with it. All she has to do is call the police! They'd come and take him away, and it would all be over and done with. But she refuses. So what am I supposed to do?"

Oy! Would that it were so simple. Here's what could actually happen if his patient were to call the police. The police might come to the house but be forced to turn around and leave because they find no evidence of abuse. Some abusers have an amazing ability to switch off their rage (proving that it isn't rage at all but a control tactic) and present a calm face to police officers. While he sits on the sofa, relaxed and smiling, his victim, red-faced, screaming, and disheveled, looks like a crazed lunatic. And he, cool as a cucumber, says, "I'm sorry, officers. She gets like this when it's her time of the month." Or the cops *do* find evidence, and her husband even gets locked up for the night. Then he's out the next day, furious with her for getting him into trouble. Or, the case *does* get to court, but by that time her husband has apologized, threatened to fight for custody, or threatened to tell Child Protective Services that she is an unfit mother, she won't testify against him. Since the case probably hinges on her testimony, the prosecutor has no alternative but to drop the charges. Or she and the arresting officer *do* testify against him, but his lawyer convinces the judge or jury that his client's assault was a minor transgression, merely a marital spat gone haywire, and he receives a light jail sentence. Or probation. Or nothing whatsoever. Shockingly, less than two percent of all abusers ever serve jail time.

It is important to understand the point of view of the police, as well. I have enormous respect for police officers. A cop goes to a great deal of trouble to go to the house, collect evidence, arrest the batterer, offer compassion to the victim, build a case, prepare a report, and appear in court. Then the batterer hires a lawyer, the victim refuses to testify, and the case is dismissed or the batterer is found not guilty. After enough cases end like this, it's understandable that police and prosecutors become frustrated with the whole sorry mess.

If you want to help your friend or relative, you need to know that women who don't call the police are not idiots. Many abused women have discovered from prior experience that dialing 9-1-1 is no guarantee life will get better. The police are not always responsive. Punishment is not always forthcoming.

However, the picture is becoming less bleak every year. Across the country, there has been a big jump in domestic violence legislation. Training for police officers is mandatory in many jurisdictions. They learn how to handle a call, how to conduct an investigation, and how to write an effective report. Some cities even have specially-trained police officers that take all the domestic violence calls. With greater understanding of domestic abuse comes greater compassion for its victims.

One way you can support your family member or friend is to find out how her city or town handles domestic violence cases. If she knows that the police in her community are likely to respond appropriately when she calls for help, she may be more willing to make that call.

Legal Resources

Your family member or friend does not have to face the legal system alone, and you do not have to do it for her. Many cities and towns have victim advocates who work alongside law enforcement to help a victim navigate the complex labyrinth of the judicial system.

For a victim of domestic abuse, the legal system can be a confusing and frightening place. Most abused women have had no prior experience of the court system. Already fragile and vulnerable from the violence at home, they can find themselves lost in the complexities of a system that appears unsympathetic and filled with contradictions. Working with a well-trained victim advocate can make all the difference in the world.

Laws vary across the country. If you want to become involved as your friend or relative works to protect herself legally, it is important for you to learn which laws apply in her state. In most places, she can protect herself in three ways: by filing a civil protection order that requires her batterer to stop abusing, threatening, stalking, or harassing her; by criminally prosecuting the batterer; or—if she is married—by obtaining a divorce or separation from her abusive husband. Depending on her situation and the laws of her state, she may want to make use of one, two, or all three of these legal remedies.

Ideally, all parts of the legal system—police, lawyers, and judges—should understand why abused women find it so difficult to break free of their situations and regain control over their lives. The various legal entities should work together to protect victims of domestic abuse during a crisis and over the long term. This is the way it *ought* to work, but even though the legal system has improved, it doesn't always work as well as it should. Victims of domestic violence are still denied adequate protective orders. Convicted batterers still get custody of their children. They still receive light jail sentences or no punishment at all. Your family member or friend might have had a prior experience with the legal system that was disappointing, ineffective, or downright horrifying. She may be reluctant to try again, and this is understandable.

Even if she is not yet ready to take the legal route, you can help her build her case. Police need evidence. Police logs, medical records, photographs, and the testimony of neighbors or other witnesses who heard or saw a violent episode can all provide proof of her claim in the event of a court case. This is especially important if she is afraid of a child custody dispute. (Abusive men are much more likely than nonabusers to seek sole custody of their children. Now that you understand the dynamics of domestic abuse, you can understand why this is so; a custody battle is one more way for an abuser to control his victim. She may have left him, but he can still get at her through their children.) If his attack leaves her with visible injuries, you can suggest that she go to the emergency room and get a photograph and description placed in her medical record. If she is afraid to do so for fear of making her abuser even angrier, you can take a photo or a video of her injury. You can also encourage her to keep a journal where she records each episode of abuse. If she eventually needs to take legal action, your behind-the-scenes support will have been invaluable.

Shelter Resources
Shelters designed specifically for victims of domestic violence were virtually nonexistent in the United States before the 1970s. You may

be as stunned by this as I was when I first heard it. Although the decade was not in the recent past, it was not precisely the Dark Ages. Where did battered women go before that time? They found shelter wherever they could, living side by side with flood and earthquake victims, alcoholics, drug addicts, the impoverished, and the mentally ill.

Fortunately, the situation has improved. Shelters throughout the United States offer temporary safe haven for abused women and their children. But shelters are far more than hiding places; they are resources. They provide any number of services to women who *are not* shelter residents. Many people do not realize this about battered women's shelters; they think that unless a woman is living at a shelter, she is not eligible for shelter services. Shelter services are usually available to anyone who needs them.

Most shelters offer 24-hour crisis hotlines. Many have legal offices or offer referral to legal services. They provide safety planning and support groups for women in abusive relationships and women who have left abusers. Counselors at the shelter are also familiar with the state and local domestic violence laws. Even if a shelter does not have someone on staff to provide legal advice, counselors can provide a link to those who do.

The main purpose of a shelter, of course, is to keep women safe. In large towns and cities, the shelter location may be a closely-guarded secret, a hidden fortress protecting the inhabitants from the men who might otherwise hunt them down. In a small town or rural community, this secrecy is not possible; a woman in real danger may need to flee to a shelter in another part of the state. Like the underground railroad in the decades before the Civil War, all local shelters have provisions for this. For example, in the state of Utah, where I live, shelters in isolated rural towns frequently send women to shelters in other small Utah towns or to their counterparts in nearby states. Conversely, our shelters take in women from distant states, women whose abusers might not think to track them down in Utah. Other communities rely on a safe home network, where various families in the community house a battered woman and her children.

The National Coalition Against Domestic Violence estimates that for every woman who moves into a battered women's shelter, three are turned away for lack of space. (This is why domestic violence survivors—and their friends and relatives—often choose to support local shelters with donations of clothing, household goods, or financial contributions. I do, too. And so can you.) If you want to help your relative or friend, gather all the information about local shelters long before she needs it. Shelters fill up. You don't want her turned away during a crisis.

Living in a shelter is not the only option for a woman who is attempting to escape from an abuser. For some women, it is not even the best option. Entering a new environment that involves group living with many other women and children, with little or no privacy, with a plethora of rules inherent in a group-living situation, is not an option that any woman would embrace. But a victim of domestic violence should always know about the battered women's shelter in her area. She may not think she qualifies because she does not consider herself a "real battered woman." One woman told me, "They'd laugh at me because I've never been beaten up really badly." The people who work in shelters don't laugh at domestic abuse. They take every case seriously.

An abused woman will typically not go to her local shelter until there is an emergency. She has just experienced a violent attack, she is in physical or emotional pain, and, if she has children, she is trying to soothe their fears. You do not want your friend or relative in the position of being forced to investigate the shelter on the night she needs it—the night she is running for her life. You can help her by getting to know her local shelter well in advance. Find out how many days she and her children would be permitted to stay. Suggest that she make an advance visit to the shelter so that she—and you—are familiar with the staff and the facility. Find out what other emergency provisions the shelter can make if they reach capacity. She may never use this information, but there may come a time when it will save her life.

Counseling Resources

Counseling for women in abusive relationships is a tricky business. Your initial thought might be that she and her partner need couples therapy or marriage counseling. At first glance, this appears logical. After all, this is a couple that seems to be having problems, so wouldn't couples counseling be the best way to help them sort out their problems? For most troubled relationships, this would be true. But it is *not* true for abusive relationships.

Couples therapy is based on two underlying assumptions. The first is that there is equality between the partners. The second is that each partner contributes to creating the problems in the relationship. These assumptions simply are not true in an abusive relationship. His abuse is not related to her actions. It doesn't matter what she does; he'll always find a way that she's doing it wrong. But he keeps telling her (and he probably even believes, at some level) that his behavior is her fault, that if she only were taller, shorter, sexier, not such a slut, a more attentive mother or a less protective mother, he would treat her well. And by the time the two of them get to a therapist's office, *she* probably believes it's her fault, too. So, when the therapist asks her to examine what she is doing to contribute to their problems, she'll do it. She'll examine it, by golly, until she's blue in the face. Meanwhile, her husband has just gotten support for what he's been saying all along— she is causing this.

Couples therapy is also inappropriate because it can be dangerous for the victim. As you have learned, there are abnormal power and control dynamics in an abusive relationship. These make it impossible for the victim to be honest in the sessions. If she tells the therapist what is really going on at home, she may be in trouble. Many victims report serious assaults after a session where abuse was discussed. Therapists who don't understand domestic abuse will accuse an abused woman of lying or, my personal gripe, being in denial. But in many cases, she can't be honest because if she is, she knows she'll get hurt. This is why therapists who understand the dynamics of domestic abuse will *never* see a couple together if they suspect the relationship is abusive. Unfortunately, some therapists, unaware that domestic abuse is a lot more than a black eye, offer couples therapy when they shouldn't. Be wary if your family member or friend tells you that she and her partner have decided to see a counselor together. If possible, steer her away from this plan.

You may want to suggest that she see a therapist, but she needs to go alone, and she needs to know why you have made the recommendation. She is not in counseling because you think she is responsible for her partner's behavior. She is not in counseling because you think she is crazy...though her abuser may have made her believe that she is. The purpose of counseling is to give her perspective on her relationship. A therapist who truly understands the dynamics of domestic abuse can help her see her situation more clearly, guide her through the process of examining her options, and support her as she takes steps to break free.

While individual counseling can do an abused woman a world of good, it can potentially do harm if the therapist does not understand the complexities of domestic abuse. One woman I know had a therapist tell her that the next time her husband laid a hand on her, she should grab him by the arm and scream in his face. The night she did was the night he knocked her out cold. She woke up in the emergency room with a broken jaw. This is a fairly dramatic example of what can go wrong; however, it does show how important it is to work with a therapist who "gets it."

Many therapists, especially those associated with a domestic violence agency or shelter, *do* get it. As for the others, it's perfectly understandable why they don't; when they received their training, domestic violence was barely a blip on the radar screen of their graduate school curriculum. Women who seek therapy these days are finding better support from social workers, clinical psychologists, and other counselors. One woman wrote to me, "The social worker helped me to understand that it *really* wasn't my fault. I always kept telling myself it wasn't, but talking about it with her, it made me look at things in a whole new way. I saw how my husband would always twist everything around until I didn't know which end was up."

It may take some time for your friend or relative to find someone who grasps the full picture of domestic violence. You and she may need to do some shopping around. If she is connected with her local shelter, the people there can often suggest someone in a mental health clinic or in private practice. This is yet one more reason for you to establish a link with the shelter in her area. Her doctor or religious leader may also be able to make a referral. (More about this later in the chapter.) Her state's domestic violence hotline may be a source of information; although they cannot make direct referrals, they often have lists of licensed treatment providers who have been certified in domestic violence counseling.

Some abused women choose to take advantage of support groups. Battered women's shelters often provide weekly support groups for women in the community, women who have already left an abuser and women who are still deciding what to do. In many communities, a woman does not have to live in the shelter to participate in such groups. In other communities, where a shelter does not have enough money to run a group for nonresidents, a support group may be available through a church, a community clinic, or another social service agency.

Support groups offer women the opportunity to hear the stories of other women just like them and to learn that they are not alone. When they hear about other abusive men, they discover that their partners' tactics are not unique. When they hear about other women's children, they can more clearly see the impact domestic abuse is having on their own children. When they hear about other women's struggles, their own struggles often snap into focus and appear more manageable. When they hear about other women's successes, their own success seems possible and even likely.

Medical Resources

If your family member or friend has a doctor she sees regularly, this physician may be a valuable resource. Perhaps her doctor already knows that she is experiencing abuse at home; if, for example, she has come to an appointment with obvious injuries, her doctor may have asked and she may have confided. Or she attempted to explain away her bruises, but her doctor knew enough about domestic violence to see past the smoke screen. Although it is technically possible to sustain a concussion from walking into a door in the middle of the night while answering nature's call, it is highly unlikely…and certainly will not happen more than once in a lifetime.

Chances are good, though, that her doctor does not know that she is being abused. Abused women are generally reluctant to confide in their doctors. They feel ashamed, embarrassed, and guilty. They worry that the doctor will think less of them. They are afraid that the doctor will pressure them to leave the relationship and become angry if they refuse.

There was a time when these concerns may have been realistic, not because doctors did not care about their patients but because they did not have the tools to help them. But times are changing; doctors now receive training in recognizing the dynamics of domestic violence and learn how to support patients who are victims. Younger doctors learn these skills in medical school. Older doctors update their knowledge in continuing education courses. Your family member or friend may find her doctor to be a helpful resource in several ways.

First, a doctor who knows about domestic abuse can better treat her overall health. She may not have a black eye or a broken jaw, but she may have stubborn migraines, mysterious stomachaches, or persistent anxiety attacks. Any of these might be related to the stress of living under the thumb of an abuser. Without knowing her home situation, the doctor can only respond to her physical symptoms. This may result in expensive and unnecessary medical tests, inappropriate medication, and referrals to specialists. Or your family member or friend may be given a prescription for Prozac and sent on her merry way. She may truly be depressed or anxious, but unless she confides in her doctor, the professional cannot judge whether such medication is a good idea or not. For example, a woman experiencing depression may be depressed because she's trapped in a situation where she feels unable to escape her abuser. If she is able to get away, her depression may vanish. A woman who has shortness of breath and irregular heartbeats may not have an anxiety disorder; she may be in realistic terror over what her husband or boyfriend will do next. If your friend or relative is willing to discuss the physical and psychological abuse she is experiencing at home, her doctor can use this additional information to provide better medical care.

Next, a growing number of doctors have access to community resources such as social workers, advocacy groups, and shelters. Knowing that she needs them, her doctor can smooth the path to these resources. Brochures and other written materials may be available in the office. Some medical practices work closely with the local shelter or domestic violence agency; with one phone call, a trained counselor can be available to meet or talk with a patient.

Finally, many people look up to their doctors as persons of wisdom and integrity. If your family member or friend respects her doctor, then the physician's opinion carries enormous weight. Imagine the impact if she confides in her doctor and if her doctor's response is "I believe you" or "I can see that you're in a tough position" or "I've known you for a long time, and I know what a strong person you are."

Consider encouraging your friend or relative to talk to her personal physician. Another helpful resource might be her children's pediatrician or her gynecologist. It is possible that the response will be less than optimal; unfortunately, many doctors are not as knowledgeable or aware of resources as we wish they were. She needs to be prepared for this possibility and not allow it to knock her for a loop. However, given the amount of help a doctor can potentially give, this is a chance worth taking.

Religious Resources

If your family member is active in her religion, she may have already discussed her situation with her religious leader. Or she may have been reluctant to do so, fearing that she would be severely scolded for her disloyalty to her husband and sent home with the admonition to be a better wife. Unfortunately, this can happen. When it does, it can be devastating.

However, increasing numbers of religious leaders have begun to realize that domestic abuse exists in all communities of faith. They understand that they if they are to respond to domestic abuse among members of their congregation, they need to educate themselves. Many new clergy learn these skills when they receive their seminary training. Some older religious leaders receive their information through journal articles, meetings, and training programs.

I have seen big changes in the decade since I began my work in this field. Last year, I received a powerfully moving letter from a minister after I keynoted the annual meeting of the domestic violence coalition in his city. He wrote, in part, "On behalf of all clergy, I ask forgiveness for the thousands of ways clergy have fostered psychological and physical abuse, including teaching and preaching views on marriage and divorce that in my view misrepresent and misinterpret the teaching of the scriptures.... Marriages characterized by selflessness, love, understanding, and deep commitment are what clergy are trying to defend and encourage, but domestic violence, psychological and physical abuse show no favoritism. Sadly, clergy may be responsible for such abuse when they have encouraged couples to stay together or blamed the victim for the abuse. Forgive us." Letters like this energize me to continue my work. More importantly, such letters encourage me to hope that, some day everyone will see domestic abuse for the horror it is.

A religious abused woman feels trapped by her marriage vows. She looks to her religious leader to help her sort out her obligation to her marriage from her obligation to herself and her children. One woman sent me a compelling letter describing her 22-year struggle to reconcile her marriage vows with the possibility of divorce. "I was grounded in my religion as a Christian and thought divorce was out of the question. My husband was also very religious outside the home. I kept thinking that he would be touched by others at our church and that our nightmare would end. It did not. I finally decided that although God did not like divorce, neither he did he like the abuse of me and my children."

Your family member or friend may be dealing with a similar struggle. You can help by encouraging her to meet with her religious leader. The response may be disappointing; she ought to be prepared for that possibility and not let it frustrate her. But there is also the possibility that she will be spiritually and emotionally strengthened by the visit. I know a religious woman who finally spoke to her rabbi after enduring 10 years of psychological and sexual abuse. "I thought nobody knew," she told me. "I thought I was keeping it such a big secret. But when I talked to my rabbi, he told me that everyone in our synagogue could see how badly my husband treated me! It was like a big weight had lifted off my shoulders. Because it came from the rabbi, I knew it was true. I knew my husband really was abusing me and that I had a moral right—even an obligation—to fight back."

It can be a powerful thing when a religious leader, when an entire religious community, mobilizes to support a victim of domestic abuse. I had the privilege of addressing a Mormon group in a small Utah town a few years ago. Most of the participants were women, but two bishops (Mormon lay leaders) were there as well. At the end of the talk, one woman stood and told the assembled group that she was trying to get away from her husband but that he had threatened to kill her if she moved out. "You all know that we have problems in our marriage," she said. "But you don't know the rest of it." She had been afraid, she said, to tell anyone about abuse in her home. But now that they had heard my talk, she hoped they would understand that domestic violence happened in Mormon homes, that her husband's abuse wasn't her fault, and that she was in danger.

The response from the two bishops and the rest of the community was wonderful to watch. Utah has strong pioneer roots; families today carry on the tradition of supporting each other during emergencies.

The evening ended with people in little clusters—not gossiping, not accusing, but working together within the context of their faith to do whatever they could to keep this woman safe. I don't know the rest of the story; I left the next morning. But no matter what happened next, this woman was better off for having reached out to her religious community than she would have been had she kept silent. The same may be true for your family member or friend.

Measuring Success

You can say and do many things to help a family member or friend who is in an abusive relationship. Be careful, though, not to expect immediate results. This is not a tennis match where you whack the ball over the net and the person on the other side promptly whacks it back to you.

You have to rethink how you measure success. If you measure success as getting your friend or relative into a shelter tonight, or on a bus out of town tomorrow, you're setting yourself up for failure. You can't expect that the person you care about will leave the minute you take some of the actions described in this chapter. Even after you assess her danger, help her plan for safety, and assist her as she works with her community resources, she is probably not going to pick herself up, bag and baggage, and walk out the door. Or she may do exactly that, only to walk back in again a month later.

This can be unbelievably frustrating. You say *just* the right words, take *just* the right actions, cheer silently as your friend or relative ends her relationship, and then listen in dismay when she calls to explain that she has decided to give him a second chance, or a third chance…or a fourth. Abused women often leave several times before they leave for good. Don't tear your hair out. It won't help her, and you'll develop a bald spot. Take a deep breath, consider everything you know about domestic abuse, and you'll be able to see why she might go back. Remember the barriers that keep a woman trapped in domestic abuse: fear, children, money, isolation, housing, to name a few. When she leaves her abuser, these barriers do not magically vanish; she comes bump up against them.

Let's suppose, for example, that a woman packs up her two children and a few belongings, leaving behind a dog, two cats, five rose bushes, and a small but pleasant house. She works part-time as a dental hygienist, so her budget permits only a modest apartment in a townhouse complex where no pets are allowed. At first, she doesn't care…she's free! This is great! Then reality sets in. The apartment is dark, damp, and smells faintly of mildew. Strapped for cash, she extends her work hours. This means she arrives home after her children come home from school, something she swore would never happen. Meanwhile, speaking of her children, they are not having an easy time of it. They don't like their new school. They miss their friends. They miss their pets. They miss their father. They know their parents had a lot of fights, but they don't see why their mother can't forgive him. The rosy glow of freedom is starting to look a little faded.

And, just about then, her husband calls. He is soooooo sorry for everything he put her through! She was totally right; he needs help. He went to see a therapist and he plans to go again. But the therapist says that he would get better a whole lot faster if she moved back home. Won't she consider it? Won't she give him one more chance to make things right, for the sake of the children? He is truly sorry for the things he did. Won't she forgive him?

Hmmm. Forgiveness, she thinks to herself, is a good thing. It is charitable. If someone sincerely repents his actions, then it would be wrong not to forgive him. If you say you're sorry, her parents probably taught her, and if you really mean it, then all is forgiven. What sort of a monster, in the face of a sincere apology, would not forgive?

If your friend or family member goes back to her abuser, she is not a failure. Neither are you. Again, it all comes down to rethinking how you measure success. For a woman attempting to break free of domestic abuse, returning to the relationship is not a step backward…it is a step forward. Yes, he may be able to lure her back with a combination of well-crafted promises and veiled threats. Abusers are awfully good at this. But every time she leaves him, she proves to herself that she *can* leave. And every time she comes back to him, she comes back to a person—a life—that she sees with fresh eyes.

This is not to say that it is easy for you to watch her struggles. There may even come a time when it is too much for you to bear. You may, for your own sake, need to create a loving distance between you. This does not mean you have failed her; domestic abuse can take an enormous toll on the family and friends of a victim. If that time should come, speak wisely and well. Clarify your limits, how much you can give and what you are willing to do. To create a loving distance, you might consider the advice of Harriet Lerner, author of the *Dance of Connection*. She suggests saying something like this: "I love you, but we are in a place where we both need more support. I know how painful it is for you to go through this. And it's painful for me watching you go through this because I love you so much. But we need to get other people involved, because I can't do it all by myself."

I received a letter from the parents of a woman who had recently left her abusive husband and come to live with them. They were terribly worried that her husband would manage to talk her back to him and wondered what they ought to do if he succeeded. What role, they agonized, should they play in her life? Should they keep calling the sheriff for her, or should they let her escape entirely on her own? I suggested that they open the lines of communication as much as possible, planning for the possibility that she will leave several times before she leaves for good. I wrote, "If she chooses to give him another chance, hoping that he is cured, sit down with her in a loving way and set out your limits. For example, you might say, 'We care about you, and we want whatever is best for you. We can see that you think it is best for you to give David another chance. This worries us because we are afraid that you will not be safe with David. But we know it's your decision. Whatever you decide to do, we will still love you.' Be clear in your own minds what you are willing to do the next time there is an incident. If you are willing to call the police for her, then tell her so. If you are willing for her to move in with you, tell her that. If there is anything you are *unwilling* or *unable* to do, you need to make that clear as well. But emphasize that you are not angry or disgusted with her for going back to David. Emphasize that you are there for her in the future, that you are not cutting off contact. Remember how isolated she is when she is with David. He defines reality for her. She needs her family to show her another view of reality."

The Power of Words and Acts

An abused woman is a woman whose circumstances have caused her to develop a distorted view of the world. Change the circumstances, you might think, and her vision will clear, but that's not the way it works. Until her world pops back into focus, it will be difficult, if not impossible, for her to get away from her abuser.

Here is a way to think about your friend or relative's situation. Imagine living in a small cabin in the middle of the woods. Visualize a deadbolt lock on the door, heavy velvet curtains at the window. The lock may give you the sense that you are trapped, but your real enemy is those massive curtains. They block out every trace of light, keeping the interior of the cabin dark and murky. As time passes, memory shifts; you forget that the world was ever light and sunny. Your only reality exists within the four walls of the tiny cabin. But now and then an outside breeze moves a curtain aside. When that happens, you see your surroundings more clearly. If it happens enough times, you begin to remember what your life was like before you lived in the cabin. And one day you open a window and slip out.

The words you say, the time you spend listening and reflecting on what you hear, the actions you take, are never wasted. Even if she does not leave immediately, even if she leaves and returns, you have not failed. Even if there comes a time when you can no longer involve yourself in her struggles, your earlier words and actions still have power. Because when you talk, listen, and act to help her, you are like that outside breeze.

You are letting in light.

You are helping her see the reality of her world.

You are making it possible for her to open the window.

Special Circumstances: Pregnancy, Disability, Teen Dating

More Barriers Than Most

Every victim of domestic abuse faces barriers as she attempts to break free of her abuser. For some women, though, the process of escaping is especially complicated. Like all abused women, they worry about safety, childcare, money, affordable housing, health insurance, and transportation. Atop these barriers, like spiky loops of thick barbed wire, sit additional obstacles. If your family member or friend is pregnant, disabled, or a teenager, she will likely need extra support. Much of this support will come from doctors, social workers, and other community resources specifically geared toward her special needs. But it is important for you to get a sense of how her circumstances can affect her ability to handle an abusive relationship. This chapter will help you understand the problems that a pregnant, disabled, or teenaged victim of domestic abuse may face.

The Victim Is Pregnant

I find it appalling that a man would attack a pregnant woman. But it happens. Please don't misunderstand me; a peaceful man does not suddenly morph into an abusive man because his wife or girlfriend has become pregnant. Pregnancy does not cause abuse. But there is certainly a connection between the two.

The link between pregnancy and domestic abuse is not completely understood. Most pregnant women make regular visits to their obstetricians throughout their pregnancies. And obstetricians, as a group, are better trained about domestic violence than some other medical specialties. They are alert to the physical signs that suggest abuse. They know how to ask with compassion. So perhaps, since obstetricians ask their patients about abuse, they are the ones that find it. Or it may be that the victim herself speaks up when she is pregnant. The thought of bringing a child into a violent home may serve as a wake-up call for the expectant mother. Although she may have once given her abuser chance after hopeless chance to redeem himself, her pregnancy may energize her to call the police, take out a protective order, or file for divorce.

It is hard to predict what effect pregnancy will have on a particular abusive relationship. Your friend or relative's pregnancy may have no impact on her abuser's behavior. He abused her before she became pregnant, he's abusing her during her pregnancy, and he will continue to abuse her after the baby is born—business, so to speak, as usual. Or her pregnancy may bring about a temporary cease-fire; the abuser's violence may actually *decrease* when he learns that she is pregnant. Although this may appear to be good news, it can give the victim false hope that her relationship is improving. I'm sure you can see why she would embrace this hope. Pregnancy and new motherhood are vulnerable states; far better to believe that her abuser has seen the light than to face the possibility of raising a child alone.

Finally, pregnancy can cause an abuser's violence to escalate. Perhaps he has always been able to control her with essentially psychological tactics such as isolation, financial control, public humiliation, and occasional physical intimidation. He never beat her up—he never had to. Now, perhaps, he feels as though he *does* have to. Or something entirely different may be going on in the abuser's mind. There is still much about the psychology of abusers that researchers have not pinned down. I have no idea what might cause an abusive man to increase his violence against his pregnant victim; I wouldn't even care to speculate. But if your friend or relative is pregnant, you need to know that it can happen.

Whether your family member or friend has experienced an increase, a decrease, or no change in the amount of abuse in her relationship, one thing is certain: being pregnant sure doesn't make her situation any easier. For some women, pregnancy can actually be the deciding factor that pushes them to leave their abusers. One woman told me about an incident during her second pregnancy that became her turning point. The attack itself was relatively minor...assuming an act of domestic abuse can ever be called minor. But because she was pregnant when the attack occurred, it served as a catalyst. She and her husband had been married for four years. There had been some physical abuse before, never serious enough to warrant medical care and never during her first pregnancy. Here is the way she described it to me: "I was eight months pregnant. He kicked me right in the ass. You know, when you're that pregnant, you've got a baby's head pressing down there pretty heavy duty. Something about that was like... I've gotta get the hell out of here pretty quick." (She did it, too, about a month after the baby was born. When I met her, 20 years later, she had been happily remarried for 10 years and her two daughters had grown into terrific young women.)

If your friend or relative is pregnant, be alert to the possibility that her danger may increase. She may not see a doctor regularly. But when she becomes pregnant, this will change; she will have a checkup at least once a month. Because she will see a nurse, a doctor, and other medical staff many times during her pregnancy, she is likely to develop a feeling of trust that will allow her to discuss her concerns. When she does, she will probably get good advice. Many obstetricians are committed advocates for battered women and their children. Even if the doctor does not have special skills in this area, he or she may know the people in the community who do. While the abuse of a pregnant woman is shocking, she can use her pregnancy as an opportunity to connect with valuable resources.

The Victim Is Disabled

As if the thought of a man assaulting his pregnant wife or girlfriend weren't dreadful enough, imagine a man beating up a woman in a wheelchair. Now imagine what it would be like to be this man's victim: vulnerable, isolated, and dependent for care on a person who scares you.

All abusers, as you learned in Chapter 2, use a variety of psychological and physical tactics to control their partners. Abusers with disabled partners have even more tactics available to them. For example, an abuser may be "accidentally" rough when performing personal care tasks such as bathing or dressing her. He may "forget" to fill her prescriptions on time. He may be "too busy" to take her to the bathroom. He may "misplace" her medical equipment, such as a walker or a hearing aid. Worst of all, he may threaten to put her in a nursing home or psychiatric institution if she tells anyone about the abuse.

How much of this is truly abuse, and how much of it is caregiver fatigue? If your family member or friend is disabled, you need to get a sense of this before you take action. You may not be able to evaluate this on your own; it may be a job for a social worker. Although caregiver fatigue can have serious consequences, it is not the same thing as domestic abuse and it should be handled differently. To know which it is, consider any violent incident in the context of this couple's entire relationship. For example, a 75-year-old man whose wife is suffering from Alzheimer's may become so frustrated with her that he yells, slams doors, or even grabs and shakes her. Is this man an abuser? Perhaps. He may have kept her firmly under his thumb for years. Or before she became ill, he may have been a perfectly nice guy. If theirs was a peaceful, pleasant relationship before her illness, then I would hesitate to call him an abuser, though his actions may certainly constitute abuse. Arrest and arraignment might not be the answer; instead, he may desperately need the support of a social service agency. He may need time away from the house, someone to take over his wife's care on occasion, and help in learning how to deal with her illness.

In contrast, consider a man whose girlfriend has been partially deaf and speech impaired since birth. An auto accident five years ago left her with a severe limp. Because of these disabilities and hampered by a limited education, she has never acquired the job skills necessary to earn a decent living. Her boyfriend enjoys telling her that she is lucky to have found him; no other man would want to bother with a cripple. Although her intelligence level is normal, he calls her a dummy in front of his friends. He refuses to let her use the telephone, telling her that he can't abide her mumbling. He mocks her limited job skills, reminding her that she would be on welfare if he had not taken pity on her. This man does not have caregiver fatigue. He is an abuser, controlling his victim by carefully and deliberately targeting her disabilities. As a predator who cuts a weak antelope from a running herd, he may even have singled this woman out precisely because of her disabilities.

Why would a disabled woman stay with a man who treats her so badly? A woman with disabilities has a number of additional barriers that keep her trapped in an abusive relationship. She may not be able to work. She may worry that if she files for divorce, her disability will cause a judge to view her as an unfit mother and award custody of their children to her husband. Finally, her body itself may be the strongest cage of all. Unable to act physically or mentally on her own behalf, she may literally be unable to get away. For example, if she has trouble moving her legs, she might not be able to drive a car. If she is deaf, she might not have access to the telephone in an emergency. If she has a speech impairment, she might have trouble making herself understood when she tries to ask for help.

The most significant barrier, though, is isolation. Isolation can be a problem for many people with disabilities; it takes a concerted effort on their part, and on the part of their families, to overcome. In the case of an abused disabled woman, though, her abuser has no interest in overcoming her isolation. Isolation, you may remember, is a common control tactic. Abusers deliberately drive a wedge between their victims and family and friends, because these are the people who would otherwise see what was going on and stop it. If your friend or relative is disabled, she is even further isolated than other abused women. Her abuser may be her only contact with the outside world. For example, he may be the one who takes her to medical appointments. He may do the food shopping, control their bank accounts, attend parent-teacher conferences, and make all decisions about family matters. Because he is also her caregiver, she might be afraid to reach out to others for help. After all, she reasons, if he is removed from the home, she could end up with no personal care at all.

A disabled abused woman is caught between two equally frightening options. Faced with the choice of putting up with domestic abuse or having no one to care for her, it is understandable that your family member or friend might choose to continue living with her abuser. You cannot fix this; you have no control over her abuser's behavior or her disability. Instead, show her that you understand the complexities of her situation. The best way to be helpful is to recognize her dilemma. If she sees that you understand the complexities of her situation, the two of you can work together to learn where she can find support from social service agencies in her state and community.

The Victim Is a Teenager

Your high school years may be long in the past, but I'm sure you remember how tough it is to be a teenager. I still twitch the occasional twitch when I remember myself as a spectacled 13-year-old girl, more comfortable with books than boys but desperate for the latter, awkward and uncertain, deeply in awe of the girls who somehow always knew the newest dance steps and the latest clothing styles. (Although I was never a teenaged boy, my husband tells me that his teen years were, although different in the particulars, equally grim.) Things haven't changed all that much. When I listen carefully to the teens I meet these days, I learn that, though they favor different fashions and their rock stars make different sets of noises, the problems they face are essentially the same. For a teenage girl, having a boyfriend makes it all a little easier. A girl with a boyfriend feels mature. She grows in self-confidence as he showers her with attention and praise. "It's comfortable," one high school senior told me. "You always know what you'll be doing over the weekend."

Some parents disapprove of teen dating, believing that it is just asking for trouble to leave a girl, a boy, and their attendant hormones to their own devices. These parents may not precisely forbid their teenagers to go out on dates, knowing that this is a battle they are bound to lose, but they certainly frown upon it. Other parents fully approve of responsible teen dating. The vast majority of parents, I suspect, fall somewhere between the two extremes.

No matter what your position is on this debate, the fact remains that, even in the best of circumstances, teen dating carries risks. When a teen dating relationship is abusive, both the victim and the adults who care about her face complex challenges. Some are identical to those faced by adult victims of domestic abuse. Others are unique to the teen years. If your family member or friend is a teenager, it is important for you to understand the special challenges of teen dating abuse.

Challenge #1: Is It Love or Is It Abuse?

I am invited sometimes to speak to high school students about dating violence. When I see the girls and boys sitting in front of me, looking determinedly bored and world-weary, I wish I could wrap each one in a thick layer of bubble wrap and deliver him or her, unscathed, aged 27, into a loving relationship. I wish I could give these kids a checklist of warning signs, clear indicators that the persons they are dating will become physically, sexually, or psychologically abusive. A guy with a big green wart at the end of his nose will smack you if you step out of line. A girl with steel teeth and horns on her head will make your life miserable with her jealous rages.

Unfortunately, the warning signs are never as obvious as this. When I make this point to teens, I see their nods of agreement; they have already discovered for themselves the confusion inherent in dating relationships. If you have a lot of arguments, does that mean the two of you are good at communicating? If he gets jealous when you talk to another guy, does that mean he loves you? If you don't like it when he teases you, does that mean you have low self-esteem? If the two of you have had sex, does that mean he has the right to tell you how to act?

Teenagers new to the world of dating and relationships find it especially difficult to decipher their experiences. This ought not surprise us. The dance of courtship is complicated for young and old alike. Suppose a guy brings you flowers after the two of you have a fight. Doesn't that mean he's sorry for his hurtful words? Sure it does…if he's not an abuser. If he *is* an abuser, though, the argument and apology are two halves of the single pattern of control. How can you tell the difference? I'm not sure.

It is difficult to interpret current events in a relationship until you look back on them. The past only makes sense seen in the light of the present. For example, my husband Neal has always dreamed of sitting down at the piano and playing cocktail music. (Which is sad, because to say he has a tin ear is to overstate his ability as a pianist.) When we were in our late t20s and dating, he once wistfully described a fantasy where he was seated at a grand piano, wearing a velvet smoking jacket, and noodling dreamy tunes while a sultry blonde in a low-cut black velvet dress draped herself across his shoulders. I suspect the most lustful part of the fantasy was the ability to play the music rather than the blonde, but that's beside the point. The point is that I had a tiny flicker of doubt when he shared this vision with me. Did the story mean that this man had the propensity to be a womanizer? No, it didn't. Neal has never given me cause to doubt his faithfulness. In retrospect, the event, which might have meant everything, meant nothing. But had our marriage been punctuated with affairs, I would have tortured myself with the piano-girl fantasy, berating myself for not having recognized the warning signs.

Even obviously troublesome moments are open to interpretation, especially for teens with limited dating experience. Suppose a girl's date behaves badly at a social event. Can she brush it off as an insignificant incident, or should she view it as a warning sign of worse behavior to come? One young woman, describing her boyfriend's behavior at a party, wrote, "He got *so* incredibly trashed, because hey, open bar! So he kept ditching me to go talk to some of his friends, and he kept drinking and he got really obnoxious. Like, we would be dancing, and he would literally pick me up and start whirling me around on the floor. I was wearing my all-purpose navy wrap dress and I didn't *really* want to flash everyone there when my dress flew up, so I kept digging my nails into his hand and his neck." If the writer of this letter were my daughter, I'd tell her to drop this guy like a hot potato. Get drunk and abandon my kid at a party? Whirl her around the dance floor until her dress flies up? I don't think so! But if she defended him, telling me that I simply didn't understand true love, I probably could not change her mind. And I would have no way of knowing whether her boyfriend is an abusive guy, an obnoxious guy, or simply a nice fellow who got drunk one night and acted like a complete fool.

I encourage my teen audiences to write their questions on index cards, saving them the embarrassment of posing their questions out loud. One high school girl's card read, "If we realize right away that it might be bad, how do we respond to the pressure of mother, friends, and the guy telling you to keep dating when you know you just want to stop it and forget about it? How do you just call it quits when it is just warning signs that you *think* you picked out?" How, indeed, especially if the warning signs can be, as they frequently are, open to interpretation. No green wart, no steel teeth, nothing but a vague feeling of unease. There is no easy answer to this girl's question. Short of sending every girl and boy to his or her individual planet when puberty descends, the best we adults can do is to teach teenagers the skill of evaluating their relationships.

Challenge #2: Helping Teens Evaluate Relationships

This is another challenge of teen dating, how to protect teens from dating abuse without stifling them entirely. Every adult was once a teenager whose heart got broken by another teenager. It hurt, but (we fondly recall, safe and cozy in the thought that we never have to be 16 again) we are all the better for it. Much as I like the idea of bubble wrap, the fact is that dating relationships are an important part of growing up. Such relationships help teenagers learn about themselves: who they are, how they want to be seen by others, what they want to accomplish in life. Relationships also help teens learn about others: what kind of people they want to spend time with, and what qualities matter in a person. Finally, dating relationships help teens learn how to work with other people to build trust, respect, and affection. These are the advantages of dating. The disadvantage of dating is that these lessons are often learned painfully.

At some point in their dating years, teenagers may find themselves in a relationship that, although perhaps not abusive, is difficult, hurtful, or downright unhealthy. This is equally true for gay, lesbian, bisexual, or transgender teens. Hopefully, the relationship will come to an end before both people are hurt too badly. The trick, I teach teens, is not to avoid relationships for fear of getting into a bad one but rather to use what they learn from the bad ones to steer them into a good one.

I use Checklist 8 to help teenagers understand the difference between a healthy relationship and an unhealthy one. Since relationships evolve over time, I suggest that they set aside some time once in a while to consider how they are feeling. At the start of a romance, of course, they will probably be feeling positively yummy, floating through life on a pink and fuzzy cloud of bliss. But how do they feel a month or two into the relationship? I encourage teens to trust their instincts. "If it starts to feel wrong," I tell them, "assume you're right."

Relationships, I explain, need to be put to the test. This advice is not cold and calculating, nor is it something out of a Grimm's fairy tale. If the love of your life is willing to ride a snow-white stallion for 40 days and 40 nights to bring you three golden feathers from the rare woo-woo bird, you are bound to feel flattered. The real question, though, is whether he or she is willing to give you a foot massage or do the laundry when you have had a brutal day. Only when we stay in

CHECKLIST 8: HEALTHY AND UNHEALTHY RELATIONSHIPS

SIGNS OF A HEALTHY RELATIONSHIP	SIGNS OF AN UNHEALTHY RELATIONSHIP
Negotiation and Fairness • Resolving arguments in a way that is fair to both of you. • Accepting each other's right to change. • Being willing to compromise.	**Intimidation and Coercion** • Using violence or threats during an argument. • Displaying weapons. • Threatening to commit suicide. (If I can't have you, life isn't worth living.)
Respect • Listening nonjudgmentally. • Being emotionally affirming and understanding. • Valuing opinions. • Making decisions about sexual activity and birth control that are right for both of you.	**Disrespect** • Putting you down. (Anyone with a butt like yours shouldn't wear jeans.) • Making you feel guilty. (After you hung up on me, I couldn't study and flunked the exam.) • Humiliating you in public. (Where did *that* jacket came from, the dumpster?) • Forcing you to have sex when you don't want to. (No way I raped you. You wanted it just as much as I did.)
Economic Partnership • Making money decisions together. • Ensuring that both of you benefit from financial arrangements.	**Economic Control** • Trying to talk you out of getting an education. (Why do you need to graduate? I'll always take care of you.) • Hiding information about finances so that you have to beg for money.
Honesty and Accountability • Accepting responsibility for your words and actions. • Admitting being wrong. • Talking openly and truthfully about problems.	**Minimizing, Denying, and Blaming** • Making light of problems. (Can't you take a joke?) • Telling you that you are imagining things. (You're crazy! I didn't push you — you tripped over your own big feet.) • Insisting that everything is your fault. (I wouldn't have to yell at you if you would quit being such a brat.)
Trust & Support • Supporting each other's goals in life. • Respecting each other's right to your own opinions. • Encouraging each other to grow…even if it means growing apart.	**Isolation** • Controlling who you see. (I don't want you hanging out with those friends of yours any more. They're a bad influence on you.) • Making rules about what you do. (You're spending too much time at soccer practice. It's a waste of your time.) • Using jealousy to justify actions. (I only got mad because I can't stand the thought of losing you.)

a relationship over time, evaluating it with both our head and our heart, can we begin to see it clearly.

Challenge #3: Danger Signals Are Often Subtle

The final challenge of teen dating abuse is to know it when you see it. Most teen victims, like most adult victims, do not look abused, with a black eye or a broken jaw. Whether you are the parent, teacher, older sibling, next-door neighbor, classmate, or family friend of a teenager, you may see something in her behavior that makes you feel concerned. Is it abuse, or is it something else? You don't want to be over-protective, but you can't risk turning away if she is in danger. If you are her friend, she may ignore advice from adults, but perhaps she'll listen to you.

These danger signals are adapted from the excellent book, *What Parents Need to Know About Dating Violence*, by Barrie Levy and Patricia Giggans. They refer to an abused girl who has an abusive boyfriend, but they could apply just as easily to a boy with an abusive girlfriend or to a teenager in a same-sex relationship.

- **Does she seem to be afraid of her boyfriend?** She may appear jumpy, nervous, or worried about displeasing him. You may have heard stories of his temper tantrums with others: for example, an explosive incident when he drove his fist into the wall or threw a lamp across the room. You may see evidence that she is being watched, followed, or monitored, either by her boyfriend or by his friends. He may call her cell phone or pager at all hours of the day and night to find out where she is or what she is doing.

- **Has she given up people and activities that were once important to her?** She may be spending so much time with her boyfriend, be so caught up in their relationship, that she no longer pays attention to her girlfriends. She may have stopped participating in school activities that she used to enjoy, such as playing on the soccer team or editing the school's literary magazine. All teens go through phases, of course, and it may simply be that she has genuinely lost interest in a particular activity. But be concerned if her relationship seems to be occupying all her energy and attention.

- **Has her appearance or behavior changed?** Take notice if she has changed her clothing style radically since she began dating. Her boyfriend may be encouraging her to dress in ways that are inappropriately seductive. Or his jealousy may have taught her to shun attention from other boys, leading her to wear unflattering clothes that hide her body. She may have gained or lost considerable weight. Generally peppy and outgoing, she may have taken to sleeping long hours. She may appear cranky and withdrawn, showing little pleasure and enjoyment of life. She may be drinking alcohol or using drugs as a way to cope with the relationship.

- **Does she have unexplained injuries?** Many victims of dating violence, like many victims of adult domestic violence, do not have obvious injuries. A lack of bruises does not mean that a teen's relationship is not abusive. But you need to be concerned if a normally graceful teen becomes accident-prone. Bruises, missing clumps of hair, or choke marks are common signs of physical violence. Her explanation may not match her injury. If questioned closely, she may concoct unlikely stories that grow increasing implausible.

Not that every relationship will exhibit all of these danger signals—far from it. Let me tell you about a teenager I interviewed in depth for a previous book. Whitney began dating Brad when she was 16. Brad was fond of telling her that she needed to shed at least 10 pounds of ugly fat before he would find her attractive. And so she dieted rigorously, bringing her slim frame from a respectable size six to barely a size two. Brad was also fond of inflicting little punishments upon Whitney whenever she said or did something to displease him. He would then coach her in plausible explanations for her resulting injuries; a swollen wrist could easily be attributed to a cheerleading cartwheel gone awry, a small scar on her chin to a missed soccer play, a burn mark to a bit of clumsiness at a barbecue. It took Brad's brutal rape after her final breakup with him to end Whitney's silence about the reality of their relationship.

Should her parents, teachers, and friends have noticed that Whitney had dropped two clothing sizes and seemed always to be sporting a minor bump or bruise? It is easy to say so in retrospect. But Whitney did not look like a victim. She still looked pretty much like Whitney, a bit slimmer, perhaps, and slightly more prone to accidents. Perfectly plausible adolescent behavior to anyone who is not looking for danger signals. Perhaps if Whitney's family and friends had known more about these danger signals, perhaps if they had understood that dating abuse can happen to any teenager, they could have guided her away from Brad earlier, saving Whitney considerable pain and self-doubt. (I continue to remain in touch with Whitney and can report that she has gone firmly ahead with her life. She went to college, graduated in four years, found a job she enjoyed, and got married when she turned 23. Teen dating abuse is ghastly, but it need not be a life sentence.)

Taking Action

Adult victims of domestic abuse generally keep their situation hidden from the people around them. It should come as no surprise, then, that teenage victims do the same. To some extent, keeping their life hidden from adults is an innate part of being teenagers! All teens have private feelings and experiences that they do not want exposed to the cold bright light of an adult's judgment. The difference between privacy and secrecy can be confusing to a teenager. The adults around the teenager feel equally torn. When does a teen have a right to privacy, and when does a responsible adult have the right to know? The first, most important action to help a teenage friend or relative is to establish a relationship of trust. If this is your child, of course, the two of you have a long history of ups and downs. Some parents and children communicate more easily than others do. Some find it useful to rebuild their relationship with the help of a family counselor.

If this is not your child, open communication may actually be easier; however, there may come a time when you must bring the situation to the attention of the teen's parents. If a teenager has confided in you, making you promise not to tell a soul, you are in a tough position. Ultimately, you may reluctantly decide that you must break your promise. In that case, make it clear to her that you are going to take this to her parents or other responsible adults and encourage her to come with you. (It is better to establish these ground rules up front. If she asks, "Can you keep a secret?" you can reply, "Yes, I am perfectly capable of keeping secrets. But if you tell me something that makes me afraid for your safety, I may decide that it is not in your best interest

CHECKLIST 9: HOW TEENS CAN HELP THEIR PEERS

CONCERN	HOW TO HELP
What should I do if I think that my friend is being abused?	• Tell her that you care about her and that you're worried about her. Make sure she knows that you are there for her if she ever wants to talk. You might say, "I don't want to put any pressure on you but you seem unhappy and stressed. We've been friends for a long time—is there anything I can do?"
	• Tell her why you are concerned. Refer to specific incidents you have witnessed, not to the entire relationship. You might say, "When he was so sarcastic about your makeup yesterday, I could see it really embarrassed you. Then when he grabbed your arm, it made me feel scared. I'm worried about your safety."
	• Offer to get information for her or to go with her to see a teacher, counselor, or advocate. Understand that she may not be ready yet but she will remember that you cared enough to make the offer.
	• DON'T make her feel ashamed, be judgmental, or tell her what to do. She'll end up apologizing for his behavior and dropping you as a friend.
	• DON'T say, "I just don't understand you. When are you going to see that the guy is a complete jerk? You never should have gotten yourself mixed up with him. You've just got to pick yourself up, break up with him, and get on with your life."
What should I do if I think that my friend is an abuser?	• Tell him why you are worried. Be specific about what you saw and how uncomfortable it made you feel. You might say, "I didn't like it when you told her she looked like a slut yesterday in front of all of us. Then when you grabbed her arm, it looked like you were really hurting her. If I didn't like it, I can only imagine how it made her feel."
	• Take a stand. You might say, "We've been friends for a long time, but I'm not going to sit here as your friend and watch this happen, and not say anything about it."
	• Give him a reality check. Let him know that his actions will have consequences. You might say, "You're going to lose a lot of your friends if you keep this up. And if you hurt her, you might even be arrested."

CHECKLIST 9: HOW TEENS CAN HELP THEIR PEERS, CONTINUED

CONCERN	HOW TO HELP
(continued) **What should I do if I think that my friend is an abuser?**	• Urge him to get help. He has a problem, whether he realizes it or not. He needs to talk to a knowledgeable adult: a counselor, coach, religious leader, or any other trusted adult. Offer to get information for him. • DON'T make him feel so ashamed of himself that he will reject your offers to help. You care about your friend, and you want his behavior to change. If you didn't think he has the potential to be a decent person, he probably wouldn't be your friend in the first place.
When should I bring this to an adult?	• *If you are afraid your friend is in physical danger, but she doesn't want to seek help.* Don't do it behind her back, though. Tell her you are going to an adult and then do it. • *If your friend is an abuser, and if he refuses to acknowledge that he has a problem.* Violence is a choice the abuser has made to achieve control in a relationship. If he doesn't get help now, he will continue to be abusive in future relationships.

for me to keep your secret. I hope you trust me enough that you can live with that.")

You can also help her plan for safety. If she is still in the relationship but is willing to admit that her boyfriend sometimes frightens her, you and she can talk about how she can protect herself when things get out of hand. For example, brainstorm how she can get away if her boyfriend becomes violent. Identify safe places she can go if she can't get home. Help her make a list of people she can call in emergencies. Encourage her to reconnect with her friends; the presence of other teens can be an important buffer to protect her when she is vulnerable.

Her safety is even more important if she has broken up with her boyfriend. This is one more way that teen dating violence and adult domestic violence can be the same; *her danger increases when she ends the relationship.* She may be afraid—rightly so—that he will take steps to hurt her or her family. Although an adult victim of domestic violence can protect herself by filing a protective order, in some states this option is unavailable to teens. In some states, it is the parent or legal guardian who must file for an order of protection. However, teens do have some legal protections. For example, all states have passed laws against stalking, an effective strategy to keep an abusive ex-boyfriend at a distance.

Even if her ex-boyfriend does not hurt her, he can still make her life pretty miserable. He may start rumors about her at school, have his buddies sexually harass her, or corner her friends to get information about her. He may call her cell phone in the middle of the night, begging for another chance. He may show up wherever she goes, popping up suddenly and without warning at a party, a concert, the mall, or a family outing. Again, this behavior is similar to the actions of an adult abuser, but a teenage victim will find it even more difficult to cope with. Attorney and domestic violence advocate Joan Zorza writes that a teen victim of domestic abuse "is likely to be even more accessible, being tied to her school, place of worship and other locations which he will know about. Often these cases come to the attention of truant officers because she refuses to go to school."

Do not be surprised if she caves in to the pressure and starts dating him again. She may be hooked back into the relationship because she is worried about him—he needs her, he can't live without her, he can't concentrate on sports or studies. Or she may be worried about herself—he has threatened to tell everyone about their sex life, he shows up at her job so often that she's afraid she'll get fired, his friends surround her at school and accuse her of ruining his life. Caught between her fears for him and her fears for herself, it is no wonder that the process of breaking up can feel so complicated.

If your family member or friend is a teenager, you can help by understanding the unique aspects of dating violence that make it difficult for her to end the relationship. You may even want to learn which laws are available to protect abused teens in her state. If you are her parent or responsible adult, you can help her to connect with community resources such as counseling programs that are specifically tailored to teenagers.

If a teenager is a victim of dating abuse, if a teenager is an abuser, her or his friends can be a powerful force for change. I use Checklist 9 when I teach teens about dating violence. It always generates good discussion. The language presents the victim as a girl and the abuser as a boy, but it might be the reverse. The chart also applies to gay, lesbian, or transgender teens. High school and college students across the country have taught me that they are willing and eager to help their friends. Like their adult counterparts, they simply do not always know the best way to accomplish this.

Eventually, after enough breakups and reconciliations, the relationship will probably end. One or the other of them will make a final break. After the relationship is over, a victim of teen dating violence still needs your support. The end of the relationship may leave her feeling a large hole in her social and emotional life. While she was in the relationship, she was isolated from her friends and family; now, she needs to reestablish these connections. She may need to make up lost ground at school. She may need help from the adults around her to become involved in school and social activities. Counseling can be an effective way for her to recover her sense of self. A therapist who understands the dynamics of teen dating violence can help her understand what she has been through and support her as she works to rebuild her life.

Like any victim of domestic abuse, the end of a teen dating relationship does not automatically guarantee a joyous and bountiful life. After it's over, it's not over. Whether your friend or relative is a teenager or an adult, you can continue providing important help after she escapes. The next chapter will explain what can happen after the person you care about breaks free of her abusive relationship, and what you can do to support her as she works to make sense of her experience and rebuild her life.

Remaining Involved

She's Out! Now What?

I have been privileged to meet and correspond with many women who have broken free of domestic abuse. In the world of television talk shows, these women typically are called survivors, the label transforming them from losers to winners, from helpless victims to women of valor. You have probably seen these programs. People reveal, they share, they cry, they hug. The host beams, the audience applauds, the problem is solved, and we can all turn off our TV sets, secure in the knowledge that the world is indeed a splendid place.

I fully appreciate the courage it takes for a woman to escape from domestic abuse; I greatly admire the women who do so. But I steer away from the easy optimism of survivor-speak. A woman who has survived domestic abuse is more than a survivor. Her life has sharp edges, rounded corners, flat planes, and curves. She was a little girl who liked to watch the seals at the zoo. She was a teenager who had pitched battles with her mother over how much makeup she could wear to school. She is a woman who always cries at weddings, who harbors a secret passion for silver high-heeled shoes, who has been known to eat leftover birthday cake for breakfast. She is a manicurist, a physics professor, a nurse, a kindergarten teacher, a carpenter, a sales clerk, a computer programmer, a mother, a grandmother.

The dictionary defines survival as the ability to function and prosper in spite of past difficulties. My experience has taught me that a woman who escapes from an abusive man must do far more than that. She can't just shut the door firmly in his face, square her shoulders, apply a fresh coat of lipstick, mount her shiny black steed, and ride triumphantly off into a golden sunset. Her experience outlives the experience itself. If you want to support your family member or friend, you must understand that her survival is an ongoing process because the aftermath of domestic abuse is ongoing.

I often ask women to tell me the best part about having left their abusers. Their stories bubble up and spill over, filled with renewed optimism, power, and a sense of purpose. Then I ask them to tell me the worst part...and they always do. No matter how much sunnier their lives are, there is still a shadow. You may be surprised to hear that there could be a "worst part" to ending an abusive relationship; if she leaves, then surely the worst is over? It's never that simple. A woman who has been a victim of domestic abuse—like the victim of an earthquake, a bank holdup, or a heart attack—is reshaped by the experience. She is not the woman she was before.

This makes sense when you consider the betrayals inherent in domestic abuse. An abused woman, remember, is not a masochist; if he punched her in the stomach on their first date, chances are excellent that she would not have accepted a second date. She did not fall in love with an abuser. She fell in love with a person who, to all outward appearances, looked pretty good. And then, sometimes gradually, sometimes overnight, it all changed. The man who drooled over her full figure now bemoans her pudgy thighs. The man who admired her sharp mind now criticizes her sharp tongue. The man who called her every night to say he loved her now calls her every few hours to check up on her.

Even after she ends the relationship, the effects of this betrayal will linger. If she has recently broken free of abuse, you may be able to see this clearly. If her experience of domestic abuse is long in her past, its aftermath may not be as obvious. In either case, you can be helpful by understanding that coming to terms with a history of domestic abuse is not simply a matter of leaving the man who has made her life a misery. Just as domestic abuse itself goes far beyond a curse or a slap, recovering from domestic abuse goes far beyond ending the relationship.

It is difficult to predict how your friend or relative will deal with her experience of domestic abuse. The worst may well be over, but you can't assume that her life will immediately be perfect. I appeared on a panel with Los Angeles Rabbi Steve Reuben, who framed it this way: "Moses took the slaves out of Egypt. It took a lot longer to take Egypt out of the slaves." If you want to remain involved, you need to be prepared for both the worst and the best parts of her decision to leave her abuser. Realize the challenges she may face after she leaves so you can support her. And be alert to the wonderful things that will happen so you and she can celebrate them together.

After It's Over, It's Not Over

Thank heaven, she's finally out from under his thumb! So why is she still frazzled? If the abuse happened long ago, why is she still dwelling on it? You imagine that if you left a relationship as bad as hers, you'd be celebrating—balloons, confetti, a live band, and little white cupcakes with pink frosting on top. Many friends and relatives cannot understand why the person they care about is not doing victory cart wheels. This, in turn, is frustrating for the woman who has broken free, who cannot find the words to explain. As one woman wrote to me, "My friends and family cannot understand why I put up with this for so long, and they don't realize that I feel my struggle is really just beginning. With the divorce, he is going to get ugly; he is going to air everything and anything he can about me, to win some validation for the hell he says I've put him through."

If you want to provide continued support to your family member or friend, it is important that you understand what she may think or feel after the relationship is over. No single woman will experience all these struggles. But it is important for you to know that her problems will not end on the day she walks away from her abuser. After it's over, it's not over.

Concern #1: Why Does She Keep Going Back to Him?

Your friend or relative may decide to leave her abuser, take the necessary steps to get away safely, accomplish a clean break, and never look back. Some abused women do exactly that. But many do not. The research indicates that abused women return to their abusers an average of five times before they leave for good. Although my hope for you is that your friend or relative gets away on her first try, you need to prepare yourself for the possibility that she will go back to him. It is useful to understand why.

One reason she may return to him is that she feels fragile and vulnerable, like a newly fledged peregrine falcon, teetering uncertainly on a jagged cliff edge. This is particularly true during the first six months after she leaves. It is a psychologically intense time for her. Although she has left, she is not entirely sure she can make it on her own. Remember that her abuser has put a lot of energy into convincing her that she is ugly, stupid, crazy, and clumsy. Although she knows he is wrong, there is still a niggle of concern that he might be right. She is probably dealing with the realities of life that face most divorced or separated women: limited finances, childcare logistics, few job opportunities, inadequate housing. She may be suffering from the same physical symptoms that other trauma victims experience: sleep disturbances, depression, anxiety attacks. Chances are good that she is feeling lonely. Given her vulnerable state, isn't it understandable that she is tempted to go back, especially in light of the things her abuser is probably doing.

Speaking of her abuser, his actions are the second reason she may return. Remember that she is still emotionally tied to him. Once upon a time, she loved this man, and she may still. Abusers know this, and they use it. Most abusers do not let their victims go without putting up a fight. Assume that the man who has been abusing your friend or relative will work hard to get her back because if she leaves him, then he has to face the fact that he has lost control. And control, as you now understand, is what abusers need the most.

In Chapter 2, you learned that an abuser will use a variety of physical and psychological tactics to *gain* control of the relationship. Doesn't it make sense that, if his victim tries to leave, he will also use a combination of physical and psychological tactics to *regain* control? As you can see in Checklist 10, abusers work hard to either convince their victims to come back or to make them pay dearly for having left. I have never met a woman whose husband or boyfriend did not try at least one of these tactics when she ended the relationship. Most women report that their abusers used a combination. A few abusers blitz their victims with all of them, even though some are logically inconsistent with others. He apologizes while maintaining that the problems are all her fault. He takes her to an expensive restaurant, where he first threatens to kill her and then insists that he cannot live without her.

An abuser's turnabout, undermining, manipulation, threats, or attacks can be devastating to his former victim, especially immediately after she escapes, when she is most vulnerable. Two particularly frightening abuser tactics are stalking and harassment. I consider these to be attacks rather than simply threats. *Stalking and harassment are violence from a distance.* Without speaking a word, the stalker shows his victim how easy it would be to kill her. He lets his victim see him sitting across from her workplace doing nothing more than watching her. He follows her on foot and with his car. He rides past her house over and over again. Try to imagine what it would be like to look up and see the person who scares you more than anyone in the world. Now imagine *not* seeing him but knowing he is out there.

Along with stalking comes harassment. An abuser may telephone his victim at home, at work, or on her cell phone every 15 minutes, alternating between hysterical pleadings, vile curses, sweet words, empty

---

CHECKLIST 10:
AN ABUSER USES A VARIETY OF TACTICS TO REGAIN CONTROL IF HIS VICTIM LEAVES

TACTIC	EXAMPLES
Turnabout	• He apologizes profusely and makes extravagant promises to change. • He turns super-nice, praising her to the skies or agreeing with everything she says.
Undermining	• He tells her that she is too stupid to get, or keep, a decent job. • He spreads untrue rumors about her sex life, her drinking, or her financial problems in an attempt to ruin her reputation. • He sabotages the people and places that she has found to support her (neighbor, therapist, case worker, school, church, work).
Manipulation	• He behaves in self-destructive ways (drinking too much, skipping work) so that she will feel sorry for him. • He tells his friends and relatives how miserable he is, so that they will pressure her into giving him another chance.
Threats	• He threatens to kill himself and take her (or her loved ones) with him. • He threatens anyone she tries to start a new relationship with, or anyone who is helping her.
Attacks	• He stalks and harasses her. • He destroys her property, rapes her, or assaults her.

promises, and angry threats. He may inundate her with a barrage of letters, faxes, phone messages, or e-mail. He may even place notes on her
car windshield or attach them to the door of her house. Harassment
sends the same message as stalking does: "I know where you are. I'm out
here. No matter where you go, you can't get away from me. I was able
to get close enough to your car to put a note on the windshield; next
time you go to your car, I just might be waiting for you."

Her own feelings of vulnerability, accompanied by her abuser's
actions, generate powerful emotional ties that may pull her back to her
abuser. You can be helpful by encouraging her to articulate the losses
she will experience if she leaves him and standing by her as she works
through the grief that will inevitably accompany these losses.

Concern #2: Why Does She Blame Herself?

Even if your family member or friend has managed to make a clean
break from her abuser, she many not have made a clean break from his
abuse. It is extremely common for a woman who escapes from an
abuser to beat herself up. She may take the blame for contributing to
his behavior, for not putting a firm stop to it the minute it started, and
for taking so long to end the relationship. It doesn't help when she
turns on her TV set and hears a self-help guru righteously proclaim-
ing that we choose our own pain. "I am not a victim but a student,"
my friend Tara said at dinner the other night. Well, okay, better to
learn from our tragedies than to wallow in them. But I personally
believe that all this there-are-no-accidents thinking does more harm
than good. Sometimes, bad stuff simply happens.

All of us need to believe that our world is orderly and that events
can be explained. We need a feeling of safety, trust in a benign universe. Answers restore order. With no answers, the victim of circumstances is left with a world view in which there is no order and,
therefore, no safety. This is why victims of a crime, an accident, or an
illness so often blame themselves. Absent a real answer, blaming yourself is a way to provide an explanation. If we attribute the tragedy to
something *we* did, we feel some control because perhaps we can avoid
that behavior in the future. Perhaps we are to blame, but at least we
are not helpless.

Self-blame is extremely common among abused women. As
human beings, we all want to feel that we have control. But the key

feature of domestic abuse is that the victim has *lost* control. She did not relinquish it—her abuser took it away from her. Once she ends the relationship, once she regains control over her life, she is understandably nervous about ever losing it again, which could happen! Her experience proves that outward appearances are often deceiving; a guy who acts like a pussycat might turn into a fire-breathing dragon. Shouldering the blame for her abuse becomes a way for her to regain some of the control. "If I caused it, I can fix it," she may be saying to herself. "I just have to learn from my mistakes. I have to understand the things I did wrong during the relationship, so that I'll never do them again, so I'll be safe from future abuse."

Simply saying to your friend or relative "Don't blame yourself!" will not do the trick. She must come to this realization on her own. However, you can play a role in helping her to see that blaming herself is neither accurate nor productive. For example, you might say, "You didn't do anything that any other wife or girlfriend hasn't done. Only most women don't get abused for it." You might also say, "Whatever you did, you didn't deserve the way he treated you."

Concern #3: Why Does She Have Trouble in New Relationships?

I sometimes get aggravated at parties, an occupational hazard. A fellow guest will approach, a glass of chilled Chardonnay in one hand, a paté-laden cracker in the other. "What field are you in?" my new acquaintance will ask, a standard start to benign party chatter. I explain that I write and teach about domestic violence, then brace myself for the inevitable onslaught. When it comes to relationships, everybody's an expert. As for abusive relationships, everyone has a theory. As the cracker wobbles and swerves, out come the stereotypes. "I think all those women who let themselves be abused must have seen violence when they were growing up, so they think it's normal." (*Sometimes this is true, but women from loving families are also at risk. The only thing abused women have in common is being born female.*) "Abused women have low self-esteem." (*Sure they do after years of abuse. Self-esteem is the result of domestic abuse, not its cause.*) "You know what the problem is? Violent movies and video games! That's why there's more domestic violence now than ever." (*No, there's more domestic abuse reported these days because domestic violence advocates have worked mighty hard to raise awareness of the problem.*) "If you ask me, there are just as many abusive women as there are abusive men. It's just that those feminists bang the drum louder." (*Aaaargh!*)

One stereotype, though, contains a nugget of truth. It's the "out of the frying pan, into the fire" stereotype, the one where abused women are doomed to repeat their pattern. Is it true? Do victims of domestic abuse inevitably go from one abusive relationship to another? Well, yes and no. Some women escape from one abuser, only to get tangled up with another. Some women, afraid to trust again, run from intimacy. These may seem to be polar opposites, but they are actually two responses to the same problem. The problem is this: Abused women sometimes have trouble in new intimate relationships. This is not to say that their personal life is over! Most women who break free of abuse eventually fall in love again and do just fine. It can take time, though. If your friend or relative keeps picking bad guys, or if she builds high walls and digs deep moats to keep out the nicest of men, resist your natural urge to scold, shout, tear your hair out, or throw up your hands in disgust. There are reasons why new relationships are tough for victims of domestic abuse. You can be more helpful if you understand these reasons.

Let's say she finally drops one abuser, only to start up again with another. Although they are in the minority, some women do. There are a few reasons why this might happen. Here are three: She may be someone who has made many poor choices over the years, she may be trying to undo past mistakes, or she may simply not see it coming. Let's explore these in detail.

Your family member or friend might have made any number of bad decisions throughout her life. You and everyone else who cares about her have been picking up the pieces for years. Perhaps she dropped out of high school. Maybe she drinks too much, takes drugs, or engages in risky sexual behavior. She may be unable to keep a job, pay her rent, or care properly for her children.

For a woman like this, domestic abuse is only one in an endless series of problems. If you are a close friend or relative, you have probably tried to steer her toward better choices, only to be disappointed time and again. If you and she are not close, this may be the first time you have attempted to help. In either case, you need to define your own limits. Her current crisis might be domestic violence, but her problems are far more complex. She may ultimately turn her life around. But to accomplish this, she will need to do more than change relationships; she will need to change herself. If this does not happen, there may come a time when you can no longer put energy into supporting her. You may need to create a loving distance between the two of you, making it clear that you still care about her but you have reached the limit of your ability to help.

Your friend or relative might not typically make poor choices. But after she leaves her abusive husband or boyfriend, she might pick a real doozy of a guy to take his place. She walks around in a blissful haze, blind to the warning signs that are making you twitch. He hasn't hit her, you think to yourself, but the night is young. The signs are so obvious to you. Why can't she see them? Odd as it may seem, she might lack insight about the present because she does not fully understand her past. She does not realize that she was a victim of domestic abuse. Yes, her ex-husband was nasty and cruel. He frightened her. She's glad it's over. But deep inside some secret place at her core, she believes that the problems in their relationship were her fault. I wouldn't go so far as to say that she deliberately repeats her history to create an alternative ending. But if her new boyfriend is something like her abuser, she may stick with him, hoping that this time she can get it right.

There is a third reason a formerly abused woman may find herself in another abusive relationship. Abusers are awfully hard to spot in advance, even for someone with personal experience of domestic abuse. Let me tell you about one woman whose second husband was even more abusive than her first. She never knew it because no one knew it, because he had everyone fooled. All she saw was the side of him he chose to display to the world. This woman had been divorced from her abusive first husband for nearly two years when they met. Gun-shy about relationships, she had done little dating. But this man was different. He was a brilliant trial lawyer who doted on his mother. He was involved in domestic violence awareness programs, drawing on his skills as an orator to deliver stirring public speeches about the evils of domestic abuse. He made handsome contributions to the local battered women's shelter. "I finally found my soul mate," she told me. "Someone who gets what I went through with my first husband." Then they got married, she became pregnant, and she discovered that this man had a dark side.

Here is the way she described it to me: "It was like he would just start getting really crazy, and I kept trying to be the perfect mother to his children and the perfect wife to him. But then I got pregnant, and it was a high-risk pregnancy, so I had to lie down most of the time. One night he was throwing this fit, and I got disgusted. So I said, 'If you won't act like a grownup, I'm getting out of here,' and I walked up the stairs and went into our bedroom. Well, the stairs were wooden, and after I went upstairs and lay down on the bed, he came right up those stairs after me. I'll never forget how scary that sound was. He's a big guy, a real, real big guy, and he's stomping up the stairs, and he's just madder than hell. First he came to the end of the bed and started shaking the mattress. I was scared to death, but I tried to do what a counselor once told me when I was married to my first husband; I tried to put my arms around him and love him past it. Can you imagine telling somebody to do that? But I did it. I walked over, I put my arms around him...and he picked me up and threw me across the bedroom to the opposite wall, when I was six months pregnant."

It would be easier, and infinitely more reassuring, to believe that this woman is a silly ninny, so desperate for a man that she deliberately ignored the gargantuan red flags waving over his head. I suppose it's possible; most anything is. But I don't see how she *could* have known that the articulate trial lawyer—the man who denounced wife-beaters with such compelling outrage—would be capable of throwing his pregnant wife across their bedroom.

There are several reasons why abused women flee one abuser and go directly into the arms of another, but your family member or friend may do nothing of the kind. You are so proud of her! She picked herself up, got herself out, and moved forward with her life. Good for her! Everything, you fondly imagine, will be fine. And it might. But over time, you might notice that she is doing very little dating. Or she dates plenty of men, but she manages to find something wrong with each one.

Perhaps she is simply being picky, not necessarily a bad thing. If people were pickier, I sometimes grumble to myself, the divorce rate would not be so high. But perhaps her experience of domestic abuse has left her unable to trust again. Hypervigilance, this is called, constantly having one's radar scanning the horizon.

A woman who has been a victim of domestic abuse may learn the lesson that intimate relationships are not safe. She may become acutely sensitive to nuance and shadow, sniffing out evidence, finding warning signs where none exist. One young woman who left an abusive boyfriend told me, "So many things spook me now, even the way he smelled, the cologne he used to wear. I *hate* that cologne! I hate it…I detest it. And so many men wear it. I mean, I'll smell it in the elevator, and a part of me just cringes."

If your friend or relative is spooked by something as benign as cologne, understand that she may be over-reacting to the betrayal of domestic abuse. This makes perfect sense; if she missed some warning signs the last time, she wants to make darned sure she sees them this time. The problem is that she may see warning signs where there are none. If her abuser watched 30 hours of football each weekend, she may only feel secure with a man who has a box at the opera. If her abuser wore wire-rim glasses and sported a heavy beard, she may date only clean-shaven men with 20-20 vision. If he drank heavily, she might panic if her date sips an after-dinner brandy. If he ran around with other women, she may lose it if her new boyfriend ogles an attractive stranger's tush. This may all sound pretty silly to you; after all, plenty of lovely men watch sports, grow beards, wear glasses, drink alcohol, and appreciate a shapely derriere—just as there are culture-loving, contact lens-wearing teetotalers who would never dream of having an affair…yet believe they have the right to beat their wife or girlfriend. Even if you think she is being judgmental, you can be helpful if you understand the reasons behind her hypervigilance.

One woman described it to me like this: "I've got a residual effect, and that is that I cannot be in a room with anybody who is drunk. It doesn't matter who they are, it doesn't matter how well I know them, it doesn't matter how benign a person they are. My husband, my current husband, is the nicest, gentlest, kindest man, but if he has two beers, I'm sitting forward saying, 'Ohmigod, you've had two beers!' Which I recognize is completely irrational. My husband doesn't have a drinking problem—if he had three beers he'd be asleep. But if I see him reaching for a beer I get this thing, you know, in my chest. I know it's there and I can't get past it. Because my first husband used to hit me when he was sober, but it was exacerbated when he was drunk. It's been 27 years, so I guess I'll never get over it."

If you see your friend or relative running from perfectly nice men, be patient. Do not minimize her concerns, even if they seem trivial to you. On one hand, her instincts might be letting her down. She may be hypervigilant, finding fault where there is none to be found. On the other hand, her instincts may be finely tuned, picking up on warning signs that you have missed and that she cannot articulate. Like a fox that has survived a forest fire, the faintest smell of distant smoke will trigger an alarm. Better to flee a nonexistent fire than to risk being trapped in a roaring blaze.

Letting Go

Everything on earth moves at least a little bit. Even rock. Under the skin of the earth rest the tectonic plates—enormous overlapping turtle shells of dense stone. Yet even these will shift a few inches every year. You might want to keep this in mind as you help your friend or relative work through the process of letting go.

For a woman who ends an abusive relationship, letting go requires a gradual shifting of perception. Many people do not realize this, assuming that their family member or friend ought to bounce back quickly, and are confused and concerned when she does not. As one woman wrote to me, "It is difficult and sometimes frustrating for friends and family to understand the emotions that you are experiencing since the separation. They are just so happy that you are out of this bad relationship that they can't understand the devastating effects it has had on you, and why you are still suffering and taking time to heal. It is hard to be honest about your experience, and rather humiliating to admit to them what really went on behind closed doors."

Your friend or relative may have recently escaped from an abusive relationship, or she may have left long ago before you knew her. In either case, you might have discouraged her from talking about her past, believing that the sooner she can put it behind her, the better off she will be. But past horrors have a way of coming back to haunt us if we don't deal with them. One woman described it like this: "I have been away from an abusive relationship for 15 years, married to a wonderful guy for the last 12, and the mother of an incredible 10-year-old. I never took the time to get over the abuse I put up with so long ago. I tried to move on quickly without looking back. Recently

I've discovered that I need to go back and resolve the issues that I never worked through."

Many women who break free of domestic abuse have nightmares triggered by a book, a movie, a news story, or an overheard conversation in a restaurant. Others experience flashbacks, past incidents recalled so vividly they seem to be occurring in the present. Flashbacks are a necessary part of letting go, but they can be exhausting. They are the past made fully present, the appalling events not just remembered but relived. As one woman put it, "I wasn't simply remembering our apartment; I was actually there. Everything was in place, the furniture, the wallpaper, even the quality of light." A flashback is not like watching a movie. It feels like stepping three-dimensionally into the action. As if you not only heard and saw the dinosaurs in Jurassic Park but smelled the sickly sweet vegetation and felt the terrifying heat of their breath on the back of your neck.

The process of letting go requires time to grieve. Some people believe that forgiveness is also necessary. If you want to remain involved as your family member or friend works to free herself from her history of abuse, you need to consider both of these. You can help by walking beside her during her journey. You can provide a welcoming space where she can reflect on her past and plan for her future.

Letting Go: the Importance of Grieving

Your friend or relative invested a great deal of time and energy in her relationship. She tried, sometimes for years, to get it right, never realizing that this was an impossible task, that her abuser needed her to get it wrong. She worked hard to be perfect. As she begins an independent existence, she may experience feelings of failure and emptiness. She has lost her role as a lover, companion, and partner to her husband or boyfriend. She also may feel a loss of security. Even though she was being abused, she at least knew what she was up against. Once she leaves, she must face the unknown.

I'm sure you can see why she might grieve for her losses. In fact, you may see it more clearly than she does. Since society does not perceive that leaving an abusive situation involves losses, she may not identify her feelings as those associated with mourning. Nevertheless, such feelings often are deeply felt. One woman sent me a letter that compellingly described her confusion at the grief she feels. "I am on the verge of a dream come true after 15 years of hell from my abuser. I got fit and healthy, lost weight, look great, took a job in Arizona, and bought the dream house of a lifetime. Yesterday in court the judge agreed my ex-husband will never have overnight visitation again. Elaine, the reason I'm writing is I don't understand my feelings. I thought I would be jumping for joy but instead I've come down with the blues. I'm mourning the pain my kids went through during numerous episodes at their dad's during visitation. Is this normal for battered women? Once the abuser is out of the picture and we have nothing to push back against—then depression?"

Because of social expectations to feel only anger and relief after leaving domestic abuse, grief is usually the most suppressed and misunderstood emotion. Your friend or relative may not tell you that she is grieving, but she may hint at it by saying how tired and defeated she feels. You can help by recognizing and acknowledging her grief. She may also benefit from short-term therapy. A counselor who understands domestic abuse can help her understand that depression, tears, inappropriate laughter, anxiety, agitation, and lethargy are expressions of the grief she is working through. Working with a counselor may help her to make connections between her feelings and her progress in coming to terms with the losses she has sustained—because she *has* suffered losses. The dream has died. Every one of us has dreams. It is always sad when we come to understand that a particular dream will never come true.

After grief comes acceptance, the firm feeling that she has made the right decision. She can look beyond the pain of her past to cherish her present and anticipate her future. An abused woman who has fully accepted her losses will ultimately feel more positive about herself and in control of her life.

Letting Go: the Question of Forgiveness

"I'm worried about my mom," the sweet young college student told me after I gave a guest lecture in her family studies class. "My dad was abusive toward her. They've been divorced for 12 years. But she won't forgive him. My brothers and sisters and I keep telling her she really ought to, but she refuses." As we talked, the young woman revealed that her mother has made a splendid life for herself, running a successful business and enjoying the company of her large circle of friends. More importantly, her father has never asked to be forgiven. He has never acknowledged that he was wrong, never repented, never tried to make things right. I asked her why, under the circumstance, she believes that her father is entitled to forgiveness. She looked a bit blank, then replied earnestly, "Isn't it unhealthy? I thought you couldn't go on with your life unless you forgive the people who hurt you."

The question of forgiveness is complicated. Some people believe that we cannot move forward emotionally or spiritually unless we forgive those who have mistreated us, even if they do not ask to be forgiven. Others are not so sure. I am one who does not believe that one-sided forgiveness is possible. However, this does not mean that *healing* is impossible. Some women can heal from domestic abuse even if they do not forgive their abuser. Others cannot heal unless they forgive. They *could* forgive if their abuser asked for forgiveness, but they aren't in control of that, so they are left with unhealed wounds.

When we tell an abused woman she "must" forgive her abuser, that not forgiving him is a choice that she has made, we are saying that her pain is her fault. In my mind, though, forgiving him really isn't up to her—it's up to him. I believe there can be no forgiveness unless the person who mistreated us can demonstrate three Rs: *refraining* from further harm, *repenting* of his actions, and making *restitution* for the damage he has done.

I agree with the Reverend Marie Fortune, founder and director of the Center for Prevention of Sexual and Domestic Violence, who writes that justice is a necessary prerequisite to forgiveness. She says, "Once justice has been accomplished, even in a limited way, forgiveness becomes a viable opportunity. Prior to justice, forgiveness is an empty exercise. Forgiveness before justice is 'cheap grace' and cannot contribute to authentic healing and restoration to wholeness for the victim or for the offender. It cuts the healing process short and may well perpetuate the cycle of abuse. It also undercuts the redemption of abusers by preventing them from being accountable for their abusive behavior."

What would convince your friend or relative that justice has been accomplished? First, the abuser would have to *refrain from doing further harm*. This does not simply mean stopping his physical attacks. It also means an end to his threats, manipulation, bad-mouthing, harassing, spying, and all the other tactics that punish her for having escaped. Then the abuser would have to *repent*. Repentance is not the same as remorse. Many people feel remorse for their bad deeds, remorse that they were caught, remorse that they must pay the price. Repentance is far more than saying "I'm sorry." It is derived from fundamental change. Finally, the abuser would have to *make restitution* by providing materially for those harmed by his actions. Restitution should not depend on his victim's willingness to give him another chance; it should be provided even if the relationship is over. For example, the abuser might pay for his wife and children to receive medical treatment and counseling. He might see to it that his wife receives a decent alimony and that his children attend college.

Perhaps if he refrains from further harm, repents of his abusive acts, and makes restitution, an abused woman might choose to forgive her abuser. Just remember, it's different for every person. It cannot be done lightly. It cannot be imposed by you.

Even if she manages to forgive, she will never forget what it was like to be physically and psychologically attacked by the man she once loved and trusted. Consciously or unconsciously, the memory will remain. Trying to *forget* abuse is a waste of valuable energy. More useful is to *transcend* abuse, to rise above and go beyond. "I have been described by my friends as a bird with a broken wing," one woman wrote to me. "He took away my innocence, but I am a wiser person for it, and although the wounds have taken their time to heal, I know that I am on the right road to recovery."

Even if your friend or relative cannot forgive, even though she cannot forget, there may come a time when she can let go of her anger. In many ways, anger is a useful emotion. But extended anger can be counter-productive. If you have a wound, you can care for it, bandage it, and put balm on it. Even if the wound does not fully heal, your ministrations can shrink it down to a manageable size. Anger is like rubbing salt into the wound. It keeps the wound active, painful, a constant throbbing presence.

Even after her anger fades, even after her wounds heal, she will have scars. I have a dandy one on my right knee from an operation in 1968, in the days when a torn cartilage required open surgery, a week in the hospital, and a knee that swelled to the size of a cantaloupe. The knee is fine, but the scar shines forth like a thick white worm. Every abused woman is changed by the experience. If your family member or friend can put her memories into perspective, they will no longer dominate her life. After she lets go, she can go on.

Going on: Life After Domestic Abuse

If you watch the evening news, you might have the sinking feeling that abused women can never break free from domestic abuse, but they can and they do. Women leave abusers all the time. They escape, they rebuild their lives, and they restore their spirits. The good stories are out there...we just have to listen.

You can remain involved in your friend or relative's life by taking pleasure in her good stories. These may seem minor—the freedom to play the music she likes, the ability to write checks against her own bank balance, the pleasure of relaxing in a fragrant bubble bath. A colleague who runs a support group for formerly battered women once asked each member of the group to reflect on the best part of leaving her abuser. One woman replied, "When I was with him, he would never let me eat noisy food. But now I can eat carrots and tostadas!"

Imagine what it would be like to eat every meal with the fear that an unexpected crunch might arouse your partner to anger. Then imagine the delicious feeling you would experience when, living on your own terms, your front teeth punctured the skin of an autumn-crisp apple. "After we separated," one woman told me, "I started doing things that I like to do, that I'd completely given up. I could actually sit down and read an entire book again! I learned how to do needlepoint, and learned how to spin and make baskets, and do all kinds of fun stuff." Watch for these tiny improvements in her life. Look for ways to celebrate them with her.

Domestic abuse is devastating to the woman who lives through it. It can also take a heavy toll on people like you, the family and friends who care about her. Although domestic abuse is sad, it need not be tragic. Rest assured that there is life after domestic abuse, not the same life as before but a full and rich life nonetheless. It may never be over. But it will be okay.

Cited References

Bancroft, L., and J.G. Silverman. *The Batterer as Parent*. Thousand Oaks, CA: Sage Publications, 2002.

Bancroft, L. *Why Does He DO That? Inside the Minds of Angry and Controlling Men*. New York: G.P. Putnam's Sons, 2002.

Fortune, M. "Forgiveness: The Last Step," in *Abuse and Religion: When Praying Isn't Enough*, ed. A. Horton and J. Williamson. Lexington, MA: Lexington Books, 1988.

Klein, A. "Male v. female domestic violence," in *National Bulletin on Domestic Violence Prevention*, 8(11), November 2002.

Lerner, H. *The Dance of Connection*. New York: Harper Collins, 2001.

Levy, B. and P.O. Giggans. *What Parents Need to Know About Dating Violence*. Seattle: Seal Press, 1995.

Russell, M.D. *The Sparrow*. New York: Fawcett Columbine, 1996.

Weiss, E. *Surviving Domestic Violence: Voices of Women Who Broke Free*. Volcano, CA: Volcano Press, 2000.

Wilson, K.J. *When Violence Begins at Home*. Alameda, CA: Hunter House, 1997.

Winner, Robin. *Personal communication*, 2003.

Zorza, Joan. *Personal communication*, 2003.

About the Author

Elaine Weiss is a professional educator and writer. She has interviewed hundreds of women who survived physical and psychological domestic abuse. Her first book about domestic violence, *Surviving Domestic Violence: Voices of Women Who Broke Free*, tells the stories of 12women who successfully escaped from an abusive relationship.

Dr. Weiss is an Adjunct Professor at the University of Utah School of Medicine in the Department of Family and Preventive Medicine. She teaches medical students and faculty how to recognize and support patients who are victims of domestic violence.

She also has made presentations to thousands of people across the country. She speaks to professionals who help abused women directly, including physicians, nurses, social workers, therapists, and shelter staff. She also conducts training sessions for parents, teachers, teenagers, college students, religious groups, law enforcement personnel, and business leaders.

Her essays and articles have appeared in local and national publications, as well as on domestic violence Web sites. They have also been incorporated into the teaching and counseling programs at a number of battered women's shelters.

Elaine and her husband, Neal Whitman, divide their time between Salt Lake City, Utah, and Pacific Grove, California.

In an emergency, call 911.

For information about resources in your area,
call the National Domestic Violence Hotline
(1-800-799-SAFE).

Other Books by Volcano Press

Surviving Domestic Violence: Voices of Women Who Broke Free
Elaine Weiss, Ed.D
This book tells the story of twelve women, each a victim of domestic violence. Each escaped from her abuser, reclaimed her dignity, reconstructed her life, and—rediscovered peace. Every woman who has left an abusive man, and every woman who has yet to leave, will find encouragement and hope in the voices of these twelve who broke free.
Paperback, 213 pp

Child Abuse & Neglect: Guidelines for Identification, Assessment, and Case Management
Co-edited by Marilyn Strachan Peterson, M.P.A., M.S.W. and Michael Durfee, MD
A unique compendium from 95 contributing professionals, this book will assist those working in the fields of medicine, nursing, social work, and law enforcement. Guidelines focus on the broad range of child abuse and neglect, risk factors, intervention, child fatalities, prevention, and administrative issues.
Paperback, 370 pp

Learning to Live Without Violence: A Handbook for Men
Daniel Jay Sonkin, Ph.D. and Michael Durphy, MD.
This best-selling Volcano Press manual sets the standard for the treatment of batterers by helping men to get out of the 'cycle of violence'. Included are exercises to enhance the curriculum for longer-term counseling and educational programs. This handbook is also available in Spanish and on an audiotape. See below.
Paperback, 144 pp

Aprender a Vivir Sin Violencia: Manual Para Hombres
(Learning to Live Without Violence: A Handbook for Men)
Daniel Jay Sonkin, Ph.D. and Michael Durphy, MD.
This Spanish edition was adopted by Dr. Jorge Corsi.
Paperback, 80 pp

continued on next page

Learning to Live Without Violence: A Work Tape for Men

Daniel Jay Sonkin, Ph.D. and Michael Durphy, MD.

Audio cassette tapes

Counselor's Guide to Learning to Live without Violence

Daniel Jay Sonkin, Ph.D.

"...comprehensive guide which presents the evaluation of treatment programs and the theoretical perspectives supporting them...the chapters on assessment and crisis intervention provide critically needed information...will be a valuable addition to our Naval Family Advocacy Programs."

      — Sandra Rosswork, Ph.D.
      Naval Family Advocacy Program Manager

Hardcover, 178 pp

Sourcebook for Working with Battered Women

Nancy Kilgore

This manual helps counselors, therapists and group leaders provide battered women with a sense of involvement in their own recovery. Contains lesson plans adaptable to the individual or group setting.

Paperback, 118 pp

Family Violence and Religion: An Interfaith Resource Guide

Compiled by Volcano Press Staff

Designed to assist clergy and church workers—often the first place a person turns to for help in ending an abusive relationship—to counsel abused women, their children, and abusive men. Special emphasis is placed on diverse theology and cultures, including Christian, African-American, Latino, Asian, Jewish, the elderly, rural women, and children.

Hardcover, 302 pp

continued on next page

Walking on Eggshells: Practical Counsel for Women in or Leaving a Violence Relationship

Dr. Brian K. Ogawa

"Our shelter has served many women and their children over the past ten years. Walking on Eggshells *covers all of the emotions and stages a battered woman goes through in a way that is easy to understand and relate to."*

— Cindy Westberg, Shelter Director
North Georgia Mountain Crisis Network

Paperback, 48 pp

Long Johns for a Small Chicken

Esther Silverstein Blanc and Godeane Eagle

Holding her noodle board over her head, Mama rushes into the chicken yard to rescue a small chicken whose feathers have blown off in a storm. How she sews long johns on Heltzel, who grows up to be "chief" of the chicken yard, is told in this charming true story set in pioneer Nebraska. This is a delightful childrens' book, designed to enrich the lives of the families that share it during 'reading time' at home, school and libraries.

Hardback, 32pp

For complete booklist, online ordering and updated issues related to domestic violence—visit our website www.volcanopress.com. It is continuously updated. You may also order by phone: 800.879.9636.

sales@volcanopress.com